Pacesetter

Working with Young Athletes

By

George Bunner MBE

Edited by Sara Birkinshaw

Published by
International Fun and Team Athletics

First published 2003 by International Fun and Team Athletics
17c Church Street
Frodsham
Cheshire
England
WA6 6PN

2003 International Fun and Team Athletics

Book design and typeset by Tangent Design Ltd, Manchester, England

British Library Cataloguing in Publication Data
A catalogue of this record is available from the British Library

ISBN 1-904691-00-5

George Bunner M.B.E.

George Bunner was born in the City of Liverpool in 1932 and despite a difficult start, losing his father at an early age, George was already a promising athlete as a member of Liverpool Harriers. He worked his way through night school and college to become a Chartered Electrical Engineer and eventually Managing Director of one of the largest electrical contractors in the North West of England.

As an athlete George reached a high point in 1950 when he became English AAA Junior 880 yards Champion before foreign travel curtailed his running career. George suffered the tragic loss of his wife in a car crash in 1968 that also left him severely injured and a single parent of their two infant sons. In 1971 he married his present wife Sheila and the couple had a baby daughter. Having fought back from his injuries, he rekindled his interest in athletics and with some friends decided to form an athletic club in his hometown of Frodsham, Cheshire. Realising that traditional track and field would not suit the primary school aged children in his charge, George set about creating what have become known as the Sportshall Athletics and Fun in Athletics programmes. Both of these programmes come under the title of "Sportshall". His Sportshall vision has evolved over the years and his initiatives now form a major part of the UK Athletics programme with an estimated 350,000 children taking part annually.

George Bunner has always been keen to stress the support he has gained from his friend Ron Pickering and his business partner George Uren who joined the team in 1982. He has also been keen to ensure that all Sportshall Athletes are given the right values.

The Sportshall Athletics and Fun in Athletics programmes provide a highly enjoyable way for young people to try running, jumping and throwing activities as their first steps into athletics. It gives children their first taste of fun and excitement of track and field events in a safe environment, often in areas where the lack of facilities or the weather prevents traditional outdoor activity. Following this success, an outdoor programme has been created.

The programmes emphasise the importance of team competition and fair play and the fact that taking part and trying your hardest is more important than winning alone. Above all, Sportshall Athletics is an activity that can bring together children from across the globe in competition and friendship.

George, now recognised as a leading international authority in the development of children's athletics, left the engineering profession in 1992 to work full-time in a voluntary capacity and now at over 70 years old has no plans to retire. He can still be found in his office every day developing his programmes and satisfying his passion for athletics.

Acknowledgments

I·F·T·A

For more than 30 years I have been working to give young children their own brand of athletics based on fun and team activities, work that has now been recognised throughout the UK and increasingly throughout the world. In 1991 Frank Dick, the then British Athletic Federation's Chief Coach, approached me asking me to write a suitable manual for working with children and to assist with the creation of an activity scheme for use by local authorities.

I passed many of my ideas by my friends and associates asking for their opinions and feedback and in time the original Pacesetter Manual was produced.

It has always been my intention that this original version would be updated and the task has now been completed, with the dedicated effort of Sara Birkinshaw, to produce this edition of **Pacesetter – Working With Young Athletes**.

I would like to acknowledge and thank my many friends who kindly gave guidance and opinion to help in the production of the original manual and this new version. Frank Dick was the technical editor of the original version and Julie Nithsdale and Angela Littlewood were of particular help with the sub-editing and presentation. In those early days I travelled the length and breadth of the UK with George Uren and Lesley Pilkington initiating activity programmes, which were to become the very successful UK Athletics Startrack programme.

In the production of this updated version Sara and I have been kindly assisted by Adrienne Dewhurst, Alwyn Dewhurst, Keith Hancock, Erik Little, Paddy McGrattan, Mike Morley, Edward Parsons, Zoe Parsons, Chris Smith, John Temperton, John Woodcock, George Uren and my son Ivan.

Finally, I must say a big thankyou to my dear wife Sheila who has patiently supported me throughout the years and been of invaluable assistance.

George Bunner MBE
Honorary Secretary, International Fun and Team Athletics

It is often the case that the beginner athletes are coached by beginner coaches. This is a serious mistake. Beginner athletes have very specific development needs and must be coached by those best equipped to do so.

You see if we do not get things right for the beginner athlete, we will compromise his or her development and it will be expensive in terms of time and energy to put things right later.

Frank Dick O.B.E.   The starting point in creating the quantity of quality coaches required to address this task of coaching beginners rests in the pages of this manual **Pacesetter - Working with Young Athletes**.

The Pacesetter manual captures the concept of providing the right momentum to personal development through athletics activities; prepares coaches for this extremely important role in the athlete's development continuum and sets the framework of method and practice which bridge the values and vision of the Pacesetter programme.

I feel privileged to remain associated with realising the dreams, shared with my good friend George Bunner, of creating the right climate for young athletes to grow, develop and learn.

To the readers I wish every possible success and that immense pleasure which comes with helping young people enjoy the thrill of personal discovery whilst achieving competitive goals.

To George and the international team who have made Pacesetter the shining beacon it is for athletes and coaches, I extend my warmest congratulations. More than that, I thank you for the gift your imagination and industry has brought to athletics.

Frank Dick OBE
President, European Athletic Coaches Association

A youngster's first experiences in sport set the tone for a lifetime of experience. If the experiences are positive and fun there is a very high chance they will retain a life long interest and enjoyment of physical activity. Working with youngsters aged 8 –13 years is an extremely important role in the Long Term Athlete Development process and it is therefore essential that athletics coaches are equipped with the skills and knowledge to provide this positive, fun and quality introduction.

The material contained within **Pacesetter – Working with Young Athletes** has been written specifically for those leading and coaching a large number of youngsters in a fun and developmental athletics environment. The book is intended to be a starting point, which provides both new and experienced coaches with the guidance needed to come to terms with the world of fun athletics for youngsters.

Pacesetter – Working with Young Athletes will firstly provide the coach with the responsibilities associated with coaching youngsters and the skills required for 'how' they should instruct and organise a session. The 'what' to coach is then addressed in distinct groups of events and is presented in a fun and progressive way ensuring correct techniques are adopted at an early stage. The progressions are step-by-step from the basic ABC's (Agility, Balance and Co-ordination) of physical skill development to the more formally known techniques of each event. Safety is a key factor that is emphasised throughout the book.

Within each section, new and adapted ideas are highlighted for introducing athletic events and these ideas encourage the coach to allow the youngster to learn through play. Adapting the events to the world of the youngster is key to the success of the learning process and provides a more athlete-centred approach to coaching.

The author has provided unique, innovative and fun alternative events as additional resource material for both indoor and outdoor sessions. These events include such activities as Speed Bounce, Hi-Stepper and Soft Javelin, which are all developmental to their respective disciplines.

Pacesetter – Working with Young Athletes encourages the coach to provide sessions that will develop all-round skills and ensure youngsters do not specialise in any specific event at an early age. This is supported by the inclusion of another unique feature of the book, the International Fun and Team Athletics Association's Agility Challenge Awards Tables. The Agility Challenge is divided into Triathlon, Pentathlon and Decathlon Awards in which the youngster participates in specified events and gains points for his or her performances. These are totalled to equate to one of seven levels on the Awards Table.

I·F·T·A

Offering competitive opportunities is also important to the learning process of the youngster, but the emphasis in this book is placed on assertion rather than aggression. There are many examples of competitive activities provided that are based around team competition rather than individual performances. It is not and should not be the intention to produce young individual champions in this age group, but rather to protect and guide the youngsters to maintain their interest for future years. Other features of the book include details and ideas on warm-up activities appropriate for youngsters, basic guidance on the skills associated with officiating competitions that include young athletes and information based around organising an event.

Pacesetter – Working with Young Athletes should prepare coaches with all the skills required to lead a training session for youngsters and is an ideal resource for those wishing to combine fun with the initial stages in athlete development.

Contents

I·F·T·A

Working with Young Athletes

1.1 Philosophy & Ethics

The aim of IFTA is:

> *'To develop young people socially and physically through the introduction of athletics in a fun environment.'*

The Olympics and other major championships inspire thousands of young athletes to engage in sport. It is therefore essential that these young athletes are welcomed and continually encouraged to participate from the outset. If this encouragement does not occur then they may be lost to our sport and to other sports forever and therefore have a much less healthy lifestyle. They could also lose interest if the content of the activity sessions are inappropriate. Therefore to maintain the young athletes' enthusiasm, the activities that are provided should be full of enjoyment and fun.

Pacesetter – Working with Young Athletes will act as a guide and provide assistance in making athletics attractive to young athletes aged 8–13 years. It is important that young athletes are encouraged and educated to learn from play and games activities and not through intensive training regimes. Whilst recognising that most young athletes enjoy competitive activities, competition should be limited and the emphasis placed on assertion and not aggression, it should not be the intention to produce individual champions in these young age groups, but rather to protect and guide the young athletes to sustain their interest until they are older. Young athletes from the under 13 years age group are in the skill hungry years, where good habits and sound techniques should be honed in all areas of athletic disciplines. It is therefore essential that experienced coaches as well as novice coaches work with the younger athletes.

If talented young athletes under 13 years old are specifically trained for an event it is a recognised fact that they can make dramatic improvements but this must be kept in perspective. Many factors will contribute to a young athlete's ability and account must be taken of the spurt in growth and the large variance in height and strength associated with physical development and body change. It is most important that those leading a group of young athletes in sporting activities have a sound awareness of these matters and a sympathetic approach. For many of these reasons, a talented young athlete at the age of 11 years or 12 years may not be the champion of the future. A child is neither a smaller version of a senior athlete nor a smaller version of a teenager and therefore formal athletics training should not begin until the early teens. The basics of running, jumping and throwing can be taught to the young athletes aged 8–13 years if the events are appropriately modified for them. Young athletes should be encouraged to develop all-round skills rather than pressurised into specialising in one event.

1.2 Roles & Responsibilities

It is an enormous responsibility to lead a group of young athletes in a sporting activity. The coach of a group of young athletes has a duty of care to each and every young athlete and must therefore pay attention to the following:

Give priority to the safety and welfare of the young athlete
- Ensure that the facility is free from hazards
- Use suitable equipment
- Encourage young athletes to be properly dressed and prepared
- Ensure young athletes are not carrying injuries
- Be sure that the content of the activity session is appropriate and well planned
- Protect from all forms of abuse
- Be prepared to take appropriate action after an accident
- Establish effective emergency procedures

Encourage and maintain the involvement of the young athlete in athletics
- Do not allow any discrimination
- Treat each young athlete as an individual
- Invite young athletes to be involved in their own learning
- Help to achieve realistic goals

Act as role-models
- Dress appropriately
- Be punctual
- Use simple and appropriate language
- Remain enthusiastic
- Encourage Fair Play with maximum effort

Ensure high standards and fair play
- Demonstrate respect to all those involved
- Encourage teamwork
- Appreciate their achievements
- Encourage honesty
- Deal with parental aggression and involve parents where interest is shown in helping
- Know the rules
- Continue to develop your own knowledge and skills
- Learn from others and work in teams
- Find ways to update your current knowledge
- Be willing to accept and try new ideas

Know your limitations
- If appropriate, pass on identified talent to more qualified coaches
- Only coach events in which a recognised qualification is held

1.3 Code of Practice

As a coach, it is a privilege to be entrusted with other people's young athletes and it is therefore essential that Clubs, Schools, Local Government and National Governing Bodies of Sport devise a sound Code of Practice. For those who undertake the responsibility of an athletics coach, it is important to adopt the Code of Practice provided. An example of a Code of Practice for those working with young athletes can be seen below.

Responsible Coaches of Young Athletes will:
- Adhere to an agreed Health and Safety Policy and be familiar with the contents of the Policy.
- At all times ensure that more than one person is on site with the group and preferably at least one male and one female.
- Always ensure young athletes are not left unsupervised at the end of the session.
- Never offer young athletes a ride home in their car unless accompanied by another adult.
- Never 'play the medic' unless they are qualified to carry out First Aid and ensure that First Aid cover is provided at the facilities in use. If a young athletes does require medical attention, the coach must ensure that the other children are still under adult supervision during this time period.
- Not allow young athletes who complain of injuries or of feeling unwell to participate. Check the cause of the young athlete's complaint.
- Only use safe and effective exercise procedures.
- Encourage young athletes, parents and other coaches to play by the rules.
- Encourage evaluation of their own and of others' performances to enhance understanding.
- Applaud and encourage good performances by each individual depending upon his or her own ability.
- Encourage creativity of their own running, jumping and throwing events.
- Avoid critical language and actions that will undermine a young athlete's self-esteem.
- Set a friendly, fair but firm example.
- Remember that athletics should be a fun activity for all those involved.

1.4 Play & Learn

Learning through play is a natural gift to all young athletes and 'play & learn' is intended to be the first steps into athletics for the 8–13 years age group. This is when young athletes are in the 'skill hungry' years of their lives and they will learn at an amazing rate, most of which will be learnt through play activities and from watching others.

For many young athletes this is also the age when they are trying activities away from school and home for the first time. Young athletes like to be grouped with friends and if they enjoy the sessions and feel relaxed within their group they will continue to attend for many years.

The emphasis for this age group must be on fun, the value of loyalty to friends and pride in the team and organised activities should reflect this. The activities also need to be varied as too much of the same exercise can be potentially harmful to growing bodies.

Within **Pacesetter – Working with Young Athletes** there are many examples of introducing learning a physical skill through the form of play or a game. These examples are just the starting point and the coach should use their own imagination to create new games involving a specific activity to be practised. It must be remembered that for young athletes, play is the most effective and enjoyable way to learn.

2.1 Session Organisation

Dealing with large groups of young athletes is not the same as the coaching squad situation where small numbers are guided in pursuit of a specific skill. The larger group presents a teaching situation where the leader will be developing the young athletes' co-ordination, balance, posture, agility and the beginning of movement related to physical skill. The planning and organisation of an activity session is probably the most crucial factor to actually achieving success with the young athletes. It is therefore just as important to spend time on preparation, as it is actually to deliver the session.

2.1.1 What a coach needs to know before planning the session
- The aims of the session.
- The best ways of achieving the aims. It may be worth discussing this with other coaches.
- The size and condition of the facility.
- The quantity and condition of appropriate equipment.
- The number of young athletes in the group.
- The basic safety factors, which include nearest telephone point, emergency fire exits if working indoors, first aid box location and other factors specific to the location.
- Time allocated for the session to ensure that the benefits and reasons for warm-ups and cool-downs are included.

2.1.2 Effective organisation of groups
- The coach should be prepared for young athletes arriving late and therefore try to start with a fun whole group activity. If any latecomers do arrive they can easily join in without additional organisation but punctuality should be encouraged as it is an important attribute to possess for later life.
- Start with group sizes that can be quickly increased or decreased. This will help with ensuring efficient organisation later in the session. For example, it is easy to start with groups of six as this number can be halved, or divided by three to give smaller groups.
- If the session does need to move into a team situation involving more young athletes than in the original group size, coloured bibs can be given out at the start to ensure swift changeovers.
- When splitting the group into teams it is better to use colours or countries than numbers, as sometimes young athletes in team six will feel as though they may not be as good as those in team one.
- Where the group numbers and names are known, then a division into working groups prior to the session would be very advantageous.
- If the session is part of an ongoing regular programme, try to keep to the same small groups each session. It is pointless wasting activity time every week organising and reorganising groups. Keeping the same groups will also encourage team solidarity and build new friendships. However, during competition activities the groups must all be similar ability.
- The size of the team and groups should be dependent on the intensity of the exercise and the rest required. If the groups are too small then performance will erode and if the groups are too large then there may be a Cool-Down and / or boredom effect.

2.1.3 Provide variety

- Maintain interest by varying activities but do not overdo it.
- Try to keep a regular structure to each session but introduce one or two new things each session.
- Prevent boredom by using a short time period for instruction.

2.1.4 Put the needs of the group first

- Do not try to teach skills that the group has not the ability to learn, as the young athletes will lose interest.
- Allow for different rates of learning and differences in the way young athletes learn.
- Know when and how to progress to enhance learning.

2.2 Communication

Effective communication will ensure good delivery of an activity session and may also contribute to the learning rate of a young athlete.

2.2.1 Starting out
- If the session is taking place outdoors then it is very important that the children do not face the sun.
- Instructions must be clear and simple. For example, when stopping a group tell them they must listen for the command 'stop' or the 'sound of the whistle'.
- Try to start activities without too much talk.
- Do not shout unnecessarily but ensure that the person farthest away can hear.
- Voice and body language should be enthusiastic towards the group.
- Prepare a written prompt card, if necessary, to act as a reminder of what activities are to be introduced.

2.2.2 Stopping the group
- Before the group is stopped, know exactly what to say.
- Think twice before stopping an enjoyable activity.
- Move to a position where visible to the entire group.
- Call 'stop' or 'blow a whistle'.
- Wait until everyone is quiet then give instructions – 'Silence gets Silence'.
- If the group is large it may be better to sit them down (weather conditions permitting).

Remember…
- When the whole group is stopped, it means that there is something to say to the whole group. For example, correction of a general fault or new instruction.
- Do not highlight the fact to the whole group that several individuals may be performing the activity incorrectly and therefore when helping an individual, go near to the young athlete and concentrate upon him or her but remain aware of the general group control.

2.2.3 Control and Discipline
When sessions are interesting and contain variety and activity there is often less inclination for young athletes to misbehave. To maintain discipline throughout the session the coach should:
- Try to remain calm under all forms of stress.
- Be consistent, fair and set achievable high standards.
- Try to spot potential trouble and intervene.
- In periods of high tension, try to win time by removing the young athlete from the situation and talk calmly to him or her. Do not let him or her lose face in front of friends.
- Avoid confrontation at all costs but ensure control of the young athletes.

2.2.4 Motivating youngsters
- Generous feedback and praise is helpful to young beginners.
- Always be positive and constructive and avoid negative language.
- Your own energy and enthusiasm can be infectious. When you appear lively and interested in everyone around you, they often respond with similar levels of activity. When you show interest in young athletes, if only for a few seconds, they feel a sense of recognition and belonging.
- Avoid favouritism as this may discourage others.

2.3 Demonstration

Actions speak louder than words and a high percentage of learning takes place through what is seen. An effective demonstration can help young athletes learn new skills. The following guidelines should give a few tips on 'how to give a good demonstration':

- Identify the key points you want to get across beforehand.
- The total time for explanation and demonstration should not be more than three to four minutes from beginning to end.
- The best person to act as a demonstrator is probably a member from the group of young athletes but whoever it is should agree to perform the activity in front of the group before being asked to demonstrate. Coaches should only demonstrate the skill if they are capable of performing it correctly, it can help in gaining 'street cred' with the group.
- If using a young athlete to demonstrate, observe him or her several times in performing the skill to ensure consistency in their actions before allowing the whole group to view the desirable actions.
- Set up the demonstration activity with a few in the group while others are still working. This avoids the stress of trying to get the activity going when the whole group is standing around watching. Once the demonstration group is running, stop the rest and show them the demonstration twice if possible.
- The best position from which to see a demonstration will vary depending on what is to be seen. Do not have the young athletes facing the sun or trying to hear above heavy traffic, aeroplanes or other industrial noise.
- Ensure demonstrations and explanations are carried out, where applicable, for both right and left-handed and right and left-footed young athletes.
- Practice should begin as soon as possible after the demonstration. A practice formation should be selected which allows the greatest number of participants to practise the skill safely and effectively.
- Young athletes may not immediately comprehend what is being demonstrated. Coaches will be surprised how they will practise on their own and return to the next session as 'little experts'.

2.4 Observation

As the group practises the skill, the coach should try to focus upon individual young athletes and assess the quality of their performances.

- Are they doing what was asked?
- Is the quality of the work good enough?
- Can examples of good work be seen?
- Are movements / skills becoming consistent and effective?

In the light of these observations the coach may:

1. Stop the group and correct a general fault at the appropriate time.
2. Talk to an individual and correct his or her performance.
3. If the coach is unable to demonstrate the activity or skill, one or two athletes from the group can be used to demonstrate examples of good technique to the rest of the group.
4. Continue to let the group work and go round praising, encouraging and helping individuals, if everything is progressing well.
5. Allow young athletes to work in pairs and act as observers as well as performers.

Summary of effective delivery of teaching a skill

a) Talk through the skill
b) Give a practical demonstration with brief explanation
c) Allow time for practice
d) Observe the result
e) Provide information while practice continues with assistance from peer group coaches
f) Allow time for further practice

Remember...

'Doing things right is not as important as doing the right thing'.

2.5 Contents of an Activity Session

The content of the session is yet another vital component in ensuring success with the group. When planning an athletics activity session for young athletes, the following should be encompassed:

Content	Other Considerations
Warm-Up Activities • Games • Stretching • Event Specific Drills	**Safety** **Team Work**
Main Activities • Technical • Fitness • Competition	**Simple Judging** **Fair Play**
Cool Down • Games • Stretching	

All of these will be looked at in far greater detail in later sections of the book.

3.1 Importance of Warm-Up

It is essential that young athletes learn the importance of Warm-Up before beginning any kind of more strenuous exercise. However, with young athletes aged 8–13 years, Warm-Up is more about an establishment of good habits by means of education and can be presented as a practical group activity involving discussion, demonstration and practice.

The main purpose of Warm-Up is to prepare the body and mind for activity by increasing the body and muscle temperature. In addition to the raise in temperature, there is an increase in heart rate and respiratory rate, which will increase the blood flow that in turn increases the delivery of oxygen to the muscles. Many young athletes are under the impression that a Warm-Up will prevent all injuries. It should be explained to them that a Warm-Up can protect and assist in preventing injuries, but they could still pick up an injury after completing a Warm-Up.

The Warm-Up should begin with very gentle exercise to allow a steady increase in the body and muscle temperature. This gentle exercise could take the form of a game or jogging, depending on the size of the area, and can then be followed by static stretching exercises. Static stretching improves the flexibility range of the muscles, whilst mobility exercises increase the range of movement of the limbs and can therefore assist in preventing injuries.

3.2 Use of Games

Playing games is an ideal way for young athletes to Warm-Up as they are fun and exciting. Appropriate types of games allow the aims of a Warm-Up to be achieved and also allow the coach the opportunity to identify the ability level of the young athletes and therefore group them to provide teams of similar ability in later stages of the session. In games activities there is also an opportunity to give young athletes the responsibility to act as leaders, organisers or officials.

The following games are ideal Warm-Up activities for the young athletes under 13 years old:
- Domes & Dishes
- Farmer Tag
- Tails
- Rats & Rabbits
- Push/Pull
- Under/Over Ball Relay
- Side-Side Ball Relay
- Object Relay

3.2.1 Domes & Dishes

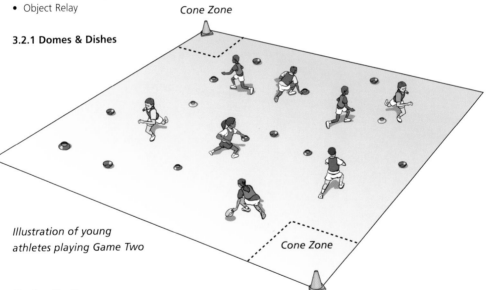

Cone Zone

Cone Zone

Illustration of young
athletes playing Game Two

Playing the Game
Place half the cones around a defined space on the floor in the normal way and the other half of the cones upside down, which creates the 'Domes' and 'Dishes' respectively. Split the group into two teams of approximately equal numbers and call one team the 'Domes' and the other team the 'Dishes'.

Game One – Cone Zone
The 'Domes' must collect all the cones that are placed the normal way and return them to their CONE ZONE and the 'Dishes' must collect all the cones upside down and return to their CONE ZONE. This is performed by the first member of each team running to collect an appropriate cone returning it to their CONE ZONE and then the second team member running to collect a cone and so on. The winning team is the one with all of their cones returned to their CONE ZONE first.

Game Two – Team Challenge

The 'Domes' must turn all the cones from the normal way to upside down and the 'Dishes' vice-versa. The team with the most cones turned over their way in a set time period (30–60 seconds) wins.

The games can be changed by:
- making number of members in a team uneven
- lengthening / shortening the time period
- increasing / decreasing the spacing between the cones
- travelling in a specific way (hopping, jumping etc.).

Equipment
- Large playing space (indoor or outdoor)
- Stopwatch
- Marker cones to use as Domes & Dishes

Safety
- Ensure cones are placed evenly around playing space.
- Advise young athletes to stay on their feet and be aware of others to avoid collisions.

3.2.2 Farmer Tag

Playing the Game

Nominate two people to be farmers and the rest of the group will become crows. The farmers must chase the crows around a defined space trying to tag as many of them as possible. Once a crow has been tagged by a farmer it becomes a scarecrow and must stand still with its arms held down by the side of its body. The other crows must then try and release the scarecrows by tapping them on the shoulder without getting touched by a farmer. If a scarecrow is released then it becomes a crow again. The farmers must try to catch as many crows and turn them into scarecrows within a set time period (30–60 seconds).

The game can be changed by:
- lengthening / shortening the time period
- increasing / decreasing the number of farmers

Equipment
- Large playing space (indoor or outdoor)
- Stopwatch
- Marker cones to define playing space

Safety
- Advise young athletes to be aware of others to avoid collisions.

3.2.3 Tails

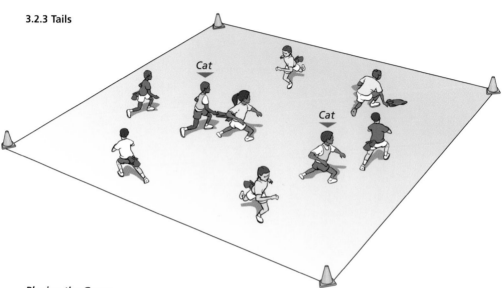

Playing the Game

Nominate two people to be cats and the rest of the group will become mice. All the mice are given a coloured band or bib (the tail), which they must tuck in to the back of their shorts and ensure that it can easily be seen and removed. The cats must chase the mice within a defined space trying to remove their tails. Once a cat has removed the tail, it must be dropped to the ground for the mouse to put back into its shorts. The cats must try and remove as many tails as possible in a set time period (30–60 seconds).

The game can be changed by:
- lengthening / shortening the time period
- increasing / decreasing the number of cats

Equipment
- Large playing space (indoor or outdoor)
- Stopwatch
- Marker cones to define playing space
- Coloured bands or bibs (one per young athlete)

Safety
- Advise young athletes to be aware of others to avoid collisions.
- Advise young athletes to take care when picking up their coloured band or bib as others will still be running around the area.

3.2.4 Rats & Rabbits
(Reaction Test)

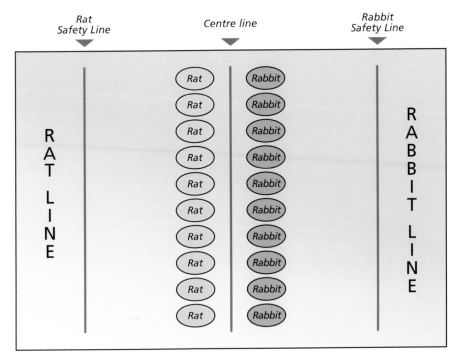

Playing the Game
Each young athlete finds a partner and they both sit on the ground approximately one metre apart, back to back, with the centre line separating them. The young athletes on the left side of the centre line are named the 'rats' and the other young athletes are named 'rabbits'. The coach calls either 'rats' or 'rabbits'. If the call is 'rats', all the 'rats' must stand up and run to their safety line before the 'rabbits' catch and tag them on the shoulder–and vice versa if the call is 'rabbits'.

Equipment
- Playing space (indoor or outdoor)
- Marker cones placed at ends (ensuring no obstruction in playing area) to define centre line and safety lines

Safety
- Ensure safety lines are distant from walls (approximately 3 metres).
- Ensure adequate spacing between each pair of rats & rabbits.

3.2.5 Push/Pull
(Throws and Thinking Test)

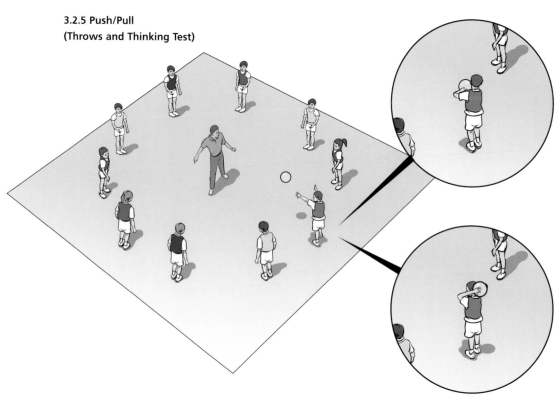

Playing the Game

The group make a large circle around the coach who has the ball. The coach throws the ball to one member of the group giving the instruction 'push' or 'pull'. If the instruction 'push' is given the young athlete must perform a chest push throw back to the coach and if the instruction 'pull' is given the young athlete must perform a two-handed overhead forward throw back to the coach. Each member of the group should be allowed a turn at returning the ball to the coach. The coach then reverses the instructions, so that when he calls 'push' the athlete should perform a two-handed overhead throw to return the ball to the coach and vice versa if the call is 'pull'. If a young athlete makes a mistake, he or she should jog around the outside of the circle until the initial starting place is reached.

Equipment
- Playing space (indoor or outdoor)
- Size 4 soccer ball initially
- Progress to 1kg medicine balls

Safety
- Ensure adequate space around the outside of the circle for young athletes to run.
- Young athlete must be aware of when the ball is been thrown towards them.

I·F·T·A

3.2.6 Over/Under Ball Relay
(Upper Body Stretching)

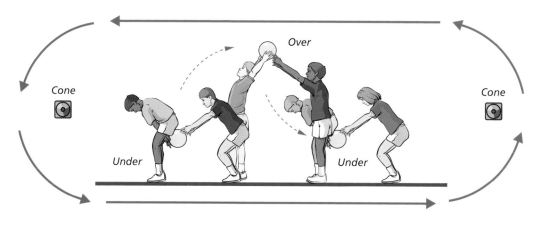

Playing the Game

The group should be split into teams of equal numbers. Each team stands in a line, with its members one behind the other and approximately one metre apart with their legs astride. The first young athlete in the team is given a size 4 soccer ball or 1kg medicine ball and must pass this with both hands over his or her head on the sound of the start whistle. The next team member takes the ball that has been passed over from the first young athlete and then passes the ball between their legs to the next young athlete.

This continues through all members of the team. The last young athlete to receive the ball runs around the cones with the ball and joins the front of the team. This continues until the young athlete who started at the front of the team is back in the original starting position.

Equipment

- Marker cones to define turning positions
- Size 4 soccer balls or 1kg medicine balls
  (one for each team)

Safety

- Young athletes should be adequately spaced apart to avoid collisions when passing the ball.
- Awareness of any balls that may have been dropped.

3.2.7 Side-Side Ball Relay
(Upper Body Stretching)

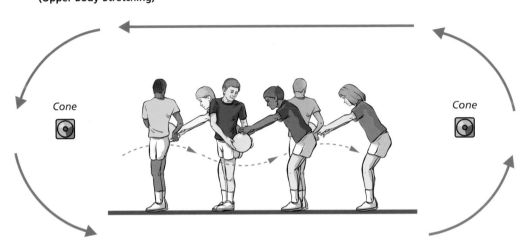

Cone

Cone

Playing the Game
The group should be split into teams of equal numbers. The team stands in a line, one behind the other and approximately 3/4 metre apart with legs slightly apart to provide a firm base.

The first young athlete in the team is given a size 4 soccer ball or 1kg medicine ball and must pass this with both hands to one side of his or her body on the sound of the start whistle. The next team member takes the ball that has been passed from the first young athlete and then rotates his or her body with the ball to pass the ball on the opposite side of the body to the next person. This continues through all members of the team. The last young athlete to receive the ball must run around the cones with the ball and join the front of the team. This continues until the young athlete who started at the front of the team is back in the original starting position.

Equipment
- Marker cones to define turning positions
- Size 4 soccer balls or 1kg medicine balls (one for each team)

Safety
- Young athletes should be adequately spaced apart to avoid collisions when passing the ball.
- Be aware of any balls that may have been dropped.

3.2.8 Object Relay
(Hand/Eye Co-ordination Test)

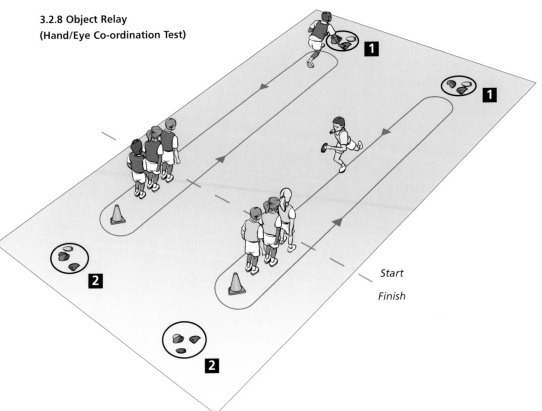

Start

Finish

Playing the Game

The group should be split into teams of equal numbers if possible. The team stands in a line, one behind the other, with the first young athlete behind the start line. On the whistle, the first young athlete runs up to hoop one, which is placed in his or her lane approximately 15 metres from the start line. He or she collects an object and returns towards the team. After running around the cone at the back of the team, the young athlete places the object in hoop two in his or her lane, touches the shoulder of the next member of the team who then proceeds to collect another object from hoop one. This continues until all the objects have been collected from hoop one and returned to hoop two.

Equipment
- Marker Cones to define turning positions
- Objects (beanbags, shuttlecocks etc.)
- Hoops

Safety
- Objects must be placed in the hoops and not thrown.

I·F·T·A

3.3 Static Stretching

Young athletes under 13 years old do not really need to carry out stretching exercises because flexibility is normally a natural ability at this age. However, right and left imbalances may exist and the need for a familiar routine in later years justifies the inclusion now. In the teenage years stretching ability quickly diminishes if not part of a regular training programme. Stretching can therefore be seen as a preventative medicine at an early age and an education to developing a very good habit.

When carrying out stretching exercises as part of the Warm-Up for a group of young athletes remember to keep the exercises simple and explain their purpose. Correct static stretching routines should include exercises for all the major muscle groups. The body is moved to a position where a muscle or group of muscles is placed under tension to perform the stretch. This position is held for approximately 10 seconds allowing the muscles to lengthen.

If the coach is working with the same group on a regular basis they may want to:
- Split the young athletes into small groups and call on each group in turn to remember a stretching exercise. This makes a 'Round Robin' game and helps them to focus on the exercises.
- In later sessions, young athletes can be appointed as leaders to conduct a Warm-Up for a small group.

The following are some examples of static stretches that can be performed as part of a Warm-Up or Cool-Down with young athletes:

Neck Stretch
Standing in a relaxed position with feet approximately shoulder width apart, to stretch the left side, gently move the right ear out and over towards the right shoulder. Hold the stretch for 10 seconds and then slowly return to the starting position. Repeat the exercise by gently moving the head to the left side.

Shoulder Stretch
Standing with feet approximately shoulder width apart, raise the right arm vertically upwards, bending at the elbow and reach down towards the spine. The left arm is then raised vertically, bending at the elbow and the left hand should hold the right arm just above the elbow.
Now hold the arm position and lift the right elbow, with relaxed breathing hold the stretch for 10 seconds. Let go of the stretch and repeat with the left arm leading.

I·F·T·A

Arm Stretch

Standing with feet approximately shoulder width apart, the arms should be as straight as possible and broughtto a position behind the back. Interlock the fingers of both hands and then slowly raise the wrists as far as possible as you exhale. Breath in a relaxed manner and hold the stretch for 10 seconds before releasing the fingers and repeating.

Upper Body Stretch

Standing with feet approximately shoulder width apart, raise the arms to shoulder level and grasp hands together. As you exhale, twist slowly from the waist to the right side to a point where the body can go no further, ensuring the hips and knees remain facing straight forward. Hold the stretch for 5 seconds and then slowly return to starting position. Repeat the exercise by slowly twisting from the waist to the left side.

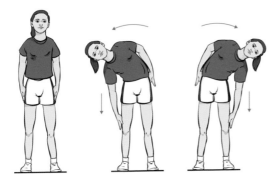

Side Bend Stretch

Stand with knees slightly bent, feet approximately shoulder width apart and arms in a relaxed position at the side of the body. Gently bend at the waist to the right side with arms remaining relaxed, ensuring that there is no bend forwards or backwards of the upper body. As the body reaches the point where it can go no further, keep the eyes focussing straight forward and hold the stretch for 10 seconds. Slowly return to the starting position and repeat the exercise to the left side.

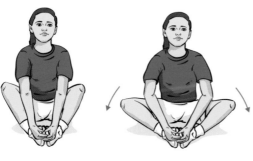

Groin Stretch

Sit on the ground with both knees bent and place the soles of the feet together. Pull the feet towards the body and allow the knees to move out to the side. Resting both hands on the feet, slowly press the knees towards the ground. Sitting on the hip bones the posture of the body must remain tall throughout. Hold the stretch for 10 seconds and gently release before repeating.

Quadricep Stretch

Standing on the left leg with the knee slightly bent, grab hold of the right ankle with the right hand and gently ease the right heel towards the buttocks. Ensure the knees are close together, the right knee is directly facing the ground and press the hips forwards. Breath in a relaxed manner and hold the stretch for 10 seconds before changing legs.

Calf Stretch

Put both hands against the wall at head height and take a step back with the left foot. The right foot should then be brought to join the left foot and then moved back a step. Both feet should remain parallel, facing towards the wall, and the right heel must be pressed towards the ground. Lean forward by bending left knee ensuring the heel remains in contact with the ground. Breath in a relaxed manner and hold the stretch for 10 seconds and repeat with right leg forward.

Hamstring Stretch

Bend the right knee ensuring the knee is directly in line with the toe of the foot. Move the left leg to a straight position in front of the body with the toes facing upwards. Rest both arms on the right leg, push the hips slightly backwards and bend slowly forwards from the waist. Breath in a relaxed manner and hold the stretch for 10 seconds before gently releasing and repeating with the right leg in a straight position in front of the body.

Providing Fun Links

- Exercises can be based around themes such as animals, objects and environment.

- Ensure correct breathing and long exhales by using simple expressions such as 'get all the air out of the balloon'.

- After familiarisation with exercises it is a great place to begin leadership skills with the young athletes conducting this part of the session.

- Ask for examples from previous sporting experiences which will provide variety and allow inclusion of safety opportunities.

3.4 Partner Work

Partner work can also be incorporated into the Warm-Up routine, however the coach must remain vigilant if using these exercises as injuries can easily occur if young athletes do not adhere to the instructions. The following exercises will be of most benefit if the young athlete is partnered with someone of similar height and build.

Throwers' Roll
This exercise should be performed slowly five times in both directions and it is also a good test of co-ordination.

Pushing Circle
The young athletes should stand facing each other at approximately arms length apart. They should then place their hands on each other's shoulders and lean forwards taking the weight. Encourage them to drive with their legs to push their partner and slowly move their feet and body in either a clockwise or anti-clockwise direction to circle round.

Pulling Circle

The young athletes should stand facing each other with their feet virtually touching. They should then take each other's hands and lean back taking the strain and slowly move their feet and body in either a clockwise or anti-clockwise direction to circle round.

Leg Lifts

One of the pair should stand with his or her back to the wall and, keeping both legs as straight as possible, raise one leg out in front. The partner should gently lift this leg to a point where the young athlete performing the exercise can feel the stretch and hold for 10 seconds before lower the leg.

3.5 Activity Specific Drills

With the first two parts of the Warm-Up carried out correctly, it is now safe to move to the third part, in which the athlete specifically prepares his or her body for the demands of the activity in the session. Activities carried out in this part of the Warm-Up routine should reflect the type of movements and actions that will be performed in the main part of the session and should therefore be more vigorous in nature. All athletes will benefit from the inclusion of activity specific drills in their Warm-Up routine as they help to focus on required movements and related cues later in the session. Activity specific drills include such things as 'Walking Tall' for sprinters and jumpers and 'Medicine Ball' work for throwers. They will be detailed further in the appropriate sections.

Walking Tall

Chest Push

Soccer Throw

3.6 Importance of Cool-Down

A Cool-Down period at the end of the session allows the heart rate and breathing rate to return to normal. It also allows the return of the blood to the heart in sufficient quantities to rid the muscles of lactic acid (a chemical result of muscular fatigue). If there is no Cool-Down period immediately after exercise, the blood can pool in the limbs instead of returning to the heart, which in turn can lead to them 'feeling heavy' and can cause nausea and dizziness.

The Cool-Down routine should consist of gentle jogging for 3 to 4 minutes followed by 6 to 7 minutes of static stretching exercises, which help the muscles to relax and prevent the soreness and tightness in the muscles. The static stretching exercises to be performed can be similar to or the same as those in the Warm-Up routine.

It is important that a Warm-Up and Cool-Down routine is always carried out even if the session is running late. This is standard good practice and the young athletes must be educated to ensure there is a life-long learning effect. It is better to shorten the main activity than eliminate the Cool-Down. This part of the session also gives the opportunity for the coach to review key points and gain feedback from the young athletes.

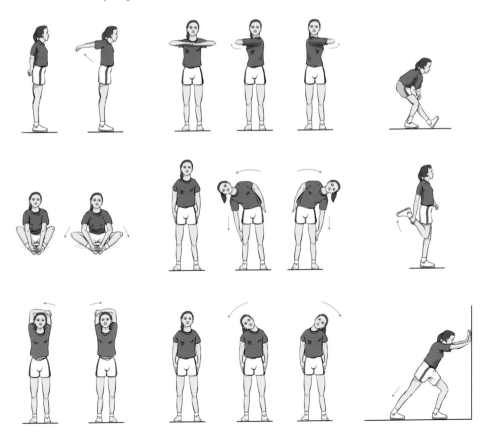

3.7 Educational Activities

There is an opportunity during coaching sessions to encourage young athletes to understand a little more about how the body works and how it can affect performance.

3.7.1 The Body As An Engine

The human body is very similar to that of a car engine in that an intake of air is required to burn fuel. In the case of the body the fuel is taken in the form of food. Burning the fuel is achieved through the intake and exhaust system of the lungs and through the circulation of the blood through the muscles.

Many of the exercises performed during 'Warm-Ups' are not only for the purposes of stretching the limbs but also to stretch the muscles surrounding the chest and ribs so that a substantial intake of air can be achieved. Explaining this reason gives purpose to many of the upper body exercises performed by track & field athletes.

Stride jumps with feet apart and then together can be performed with the arms being swung in rhythm and the hands clapped above the head. The clap is important to the exercise because the final movement pulls the rib cage up and out.

This exercise can also be performed without the clap, using very light weights (1kg) in each hand.

The different physiological needs of a sprinter, a jumper, a thrower and an endurance athlete can also be explained. They can be demonstrated by organising a partner pursuit relay around a circle of cones with one young athlete chasing another. A sprinter may be able to catch the endurance runner quickly after just a few laps. However, if he or she fails to do so, the endurance runner will gradually gain the advantage. If one young athlete catches the other, the trial is over. Please ensure a maximum of 12 laps is used for the trial.

3.7.2 Centre Of Gravity

Young athletes also need to understand the concept of the 'Centre of Gravity', which plays an important role in many different events within track & field athletics. A simple exercise to find the body's centre of gravity can be seen below.

Move arms over head

Bench

The young athlete lies on a bench on his or her front and finds the point where the body is balanced with neither forward nor backward movement. Once the body reaches the point of balance, the centre of gravity has been found. If the young athlete sweeps his or her arms forwards towards a position in front of the head, the top part of the body will then move down towards the ground.

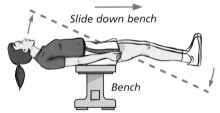

Slide down bench

Bench

The young athlete should now lie on the bench on his or her back and once again find the point where the body is balanced. If the young athlete slides down the bench with his or her lower body, the legs will move down towards the ground and the centre of gravity has then passed over the edge of the bench.

Compare the weight of a 3kg medicine ball with the weight of a young athlete. Although the medicine ball is quite heavy to lift, the young athlete's body weight can be 12 to 18 times heavier, so the legs are constantly carrying a large weight. Ask the young athlete to walk on tiptoe without a medicine ball. Lifting the body weight should be quite easy as such weight is normal to the legs. Then ask the young athlete to carry a 3kg medicine ball, holding it out in front. The legs should feel the difference when trying to move around with 3kg additional weight as more work is been done by legs and hips to stabilise the shift in the centre of gravity of the body.

Another easy exercise that highlights the difference in effort required to lift the body with additional weight is as follows. The young athlete should crouch down and then move into a standing position. Then holding the 3kg medicine ball out in front, the young athlete should be asked to perform the same task. The additional effort required by the legs to move the body weight and the medicine ball to a standing position should be quite noticeable and once again due to the effort required to stabilise the shift in the centre of gravity.

The vertical jump, explained in section 5.2.1, is a simple indicator of how far the centre of gravity has been raised from the floor.

4.1 Introduction to Throwing

The key element in throwing with a group of young athletes is the importance of safety. It is therefore crucial that young athletes adhere to the following rules at all times:

- Only throw when under supervision and when instructed to do so.
- Never throw to each other with the exception of throwing drills with soccer balls, medicine balls and primary discus.
- Do not collect implements from the throwing area if others are about to throw and only collect them when instructed to do so, after landing.
- When retrieving and carrying implements, walk do not run.
- Do not play with equipment when carrying it and if possible walk around the throw zone.
- Be aware of other athletes and activities in the vicinity.
- Stay in designated safety areas when not throwing.
- Become responsible for checking the throwing area is clear before beginning their throw.

Many young athletes incorrectly assume that the hands and arms are the key to throwing long distances. Young athletes should be taught at an early age to appreciate how certain parts of the body can provide assistance to throw long distances, specifically the legs and hips which are particularly important as they have very strong muscles. High-speed movements of the limbs can also make important contributions to the distance thrown.

A simple demonstration of showing how strong the leg muscles are compared to those of the arm muscles can be seen in the illustration below. One young athlete standing at the front holds both his arms in a bent position with his elbows pointing down to the ground and close to the body. The young athlete standing at the back cups her hands under the elbows of the front young athlete and tries to lift him using arm strength and she will find it almost impossible.

The coach then asks the young athlete standing at the front to crouch down and jump up which he should do with ease. An explanation can then be given to the young athletes that a high percentage of the bodies' weight is above the knees and the legs lifted all this weight effortlessly. Therefore, any contribution gained from the legs towards throwing will make a significant contribution to the distance thrown.

4.1.1 The Skill of Throwing

Before the young athletes are introduced to specific throwing actions, they should first be taught the skill of throwing. The simplest way to teach this is by giving each member of the group a soft ball and asking them to perform a throw using the following actions:

- Moving fingers only
- Moving fingers and wrist only
- Moving fingers, wrist and elbow only
- Moving fingers, wrist, elbow and shoulder only

When they have had several practices using the whole of the arm they should then try the following throwing actions:

- As hard as they can
- As gentle as they can
- As high as they can
- As low as they can
- Towards the ground making as loud noise as they can
- Towards the ground making as little noise as they can

From these practices the young athlete will learn effective ways of throwing to achieve specific aims.

There are two, very simple, practical exercises that will encourage young athletes to use the legs and other parts of the body when throwing for distance. These are namely the Forward Pitch and Overhead Heave, which should both be performed with either a size 4 soccer ball or 1kg medicine ball with young athletes under 13 years old.

Ⓐ The Forward Pitch is a two-handed forward throw, where the feet are positioned approximately shoulder width apart and the ball held between bent knees with the body slightly crouched. The young athlete should be encouraged to throw the ball at speed and should notice the contribution made by the legs and upper body to the distance thrown.

Ⓑ The Overhead Heave uses the same starting positions as the Forward Pitch but this time the young athlete must have his or her back to the throwing direction. The ball should be released at speed and the optimum point of release is above the head with the arms kept long.

4.1.2 Common Root Movements in Throwing

The development of throwing events in athletics is best thought of as growing from a common root movement. The common root idea is based on the fact that at their most fundamental level the Shot, Discus and Javelin involve a very similar action sequence. If the elements of the action sequence are practised and mastered, the young athlete will be well equipped to develop the skills for throwing further. The action sequence (in the right-handed thrower) is as follows:

4.1.2.1 Weight Transfer from Right to Left

The standing throw is initiated by the right (back) leg rotating the hips forward, which in turn will transfer the weight over the left (front) leg. It may be worth using the cue: Shift - Lift which means the weight should be shifted from right to left and combines with lift towards the release position. Turn the heel of the right foot to face the back of the circle and the chest will automatically move towards the throwing direction.

4.1.2.2 Legs First, Arms Last and Fast

It is important that the strong and slower-moving muscles of the lower limbs accelerate the throwing implement in the initial part of the throw. The weaker, but faster-moving muscles of the arms can only be effective when the throwing implement is moving and therefore the arms are used as late as possible.

4.1.2.3 Extension

The young athlete starts in a low position with the aim of finishing the throw in a high position. The throwing implement is therefore always released when the body and arms are in a stretched and high position. The thrower should finish by extending both legs in order that he or she stands tall.

4.1.2.4 Left Side Brace

The left side of the body should be braced to allow the right side to accelerate round or over it ensuring a strong and powerful release position. Lack of strength or misunderstanding causes many young athletes to collapse the left side of the body just before release.

4.1.3 Types of Throws

There are 4 basic types of throw which relate to the following actions:

a) Pushing

b) Pulling

c) Slinging

d) Heaving

Each of these throwing actions can denote one of the four throws that form the throws element of track & field athletics. All of these actions can be developed by having the young athletes working in pairs throwing a size 4 soccer ball to each other from the following positions:

1. Sitting

2. Kneeling

3. Standing facing the direction of the throw

4. Standing sideways to the direction of the throw

5. Introduction of run ups, glides and turns

4.2 Shot (Push)

4.2.1 Introducing the Pushing Action

The 'pushing' action of the Shot can be introduced by using a chest push, which is a two handed throw off the chest using a size 4 soccer ball or 1kg medicine ball. Both feet should remain on the floor at all times. The young athlete should be encouraged to bend his or her knees at the beginning of the throw and straighten during the throwing action to maximise the use of the legs and thus increase the distance thrown. In the above illustration the young athlete performing the activity is left-handed as the right foot is forward. For right-handed young athletes the left foot would be in the forward position. However, it may also be worth performing the exercise with the other foot forward to provide equity between the right and left side of the body for muscle strength and movement patterns.

4.2.2 Shot Put Progressions for the Standing Throw

Using a 600g primary shot a progressive action for the shot can be taught by doing a 'put' from the kneeling position. It should be noted that without being told the young athlete will normally place the opposite leg forward and knee up to the putting arm.

After the young athlete has 'put' from the kneeling position several times, he or she can then progress to a basic position for a standing 'put'. The young athlete stands up from the kneeling position and pulls the rear leg closer to the front leg as in the following illustration and performs this basic standing 'put'.

From the standing position, the young athlete turns the shoulders away from the throwing direction to achieve the chin-knee-toe position from which momentum can be gained when making the 'put'. The feet should be placed so as to give purchase to the turn and shift to allow the use of the legs. If you use the right arm to 'put' then it is the left leg that is placed forward and vice-versa if the left arm is used.

By simple practice and development of technique young athletes will quickly improve the distance 'put' as they begin to:
- use the strong muscles in the legs
- start from a low to a high position therefore ensuring the application of greater acceleration so that the object has maximum speed when it leaves the hand

Heel of right foot is in line with toes of left foot

4.2.3 How to Hold the Shot

A correct grip of the shot will assist young athletes to achieve maximum distance when they 'put'. It is important to ensure the implement to be used is not too large for the young athlete's hand and is an appropriate weight. A 600g primary shot is an advisable weight for young athletes under 11 years. The maximum weight 2.72kg for girls under 13 years old and 3.25kg for boys under 13 years old.

The young athlete should place the shot in the throwing hand at the base of the first three fingers ensuring it does not rest in the palm. The first three fingers should then be placed behind the shot, with the thumb and little finger providing support at the side. The shot should then be pushed into the neck which will ensure the elbow is held high and correctly ready to begin the 'put'.

4.2.4 Shot Put Progressions for a Moving Throw

Young athletes can experiment by trying to accelerate their body and thus the shot by moving backwards over a small area such as two lanes of an athletics track. The first moving throw that should be taught is the 'shuffle'.

To begin the 'shuffle' approach, the young athlete should face the opposite direction to which he or she is throwing. A right-handed thrower would start with the body weight on a flexed right leg with the left leg held loose. The sequence that should take place is as follows:

- Extension of the left leg, propelling the young athlete towards the direction of the throw
- Landing on the left foot the weight is transferred to the left leg
- The right leg is pulled towards the left leg transferring the weight once again to the right hand side
- Extension of the left leg and planting the foot to achieve a strong base in which the hips can be rotated
- The young athlete now turns into the throw, transferring weight from right to left. The shot is released once a forward stance, with extension of the body and throwing arm has been achieved.
- Encourage the young athlete to walk back towards the initial starting point before retrieving the shot, as this is a good habit to develop for competition purposes.

4.3 Javelin (Pull)

4.3.1 Introducing the Pulling Action

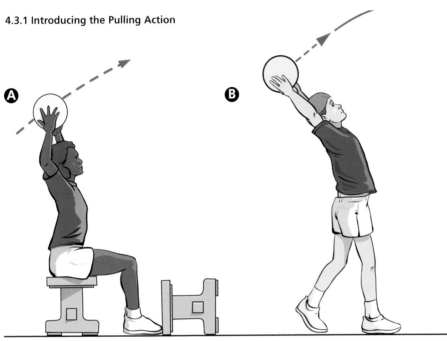

Illustration of a left-handed thrower

Ⓐ The sitting throw and soccer throw are both basic pulling throws. The sitting throw is a two-handed overhead throw using a size 4 soccer ball. The young athlete sits on a standard gym bench with both feet touching the floor and starts the throw from behind the head. The legs and hips act as anchor points so that the torso can move. The ball should be released from straight arms above the head to gain maximum throwing distance.

Ⓑ The soccer throw again is a two-handed overhead throw using either a size 4 soccer ball or 1kg medicine ball. The young athlete stands with one foot in front of the other behind the throwing line to gain purchase and starts the throw from behind the head with slightly bent arms, releasing the ball with straight arms when above the head.

Throwing a ball and throwing a javelin are somewhat related but for the purpose of teaching young athletes it is recommended that tennis balls, javelin balls, soft javelins or plastic javelins are used as safety is of paramount importance.

4.3.2 Throwing a Tennis Ball

Throwing a tennis ball, baseball, cricket ball or field hockey ball is a good outdoor event for young athletes aged 8–11. It can teach the basic skills of a javelin throw as it utilises the pulling action. Young athletes can also note from this throwing activity the disadvantage of throwing the ball too high or too low when the ball leaves the hand. Emphasis should be placed on smooth throwing rather than maximum effort due to the lightness of the ball.

4.3.3 Throwing a Javelin Ball

The javelin ball is a little bigger than a tennis ball but with the additions of a special finger grip and weight. It is predominantly used by javelin throwers during indoor winter training sessions.

4.3.4 Throwing a Soft Javelin or Plastic Javelin

The use of either soft javelins or plastic javelins is recommended as they can be used safely both indoor and outdoor for all practice requirements. The illustrations below indicate where the respective javelins should be held to achieve maximum throwing distance. When throwing these javelins the palm of the hand should be facing upwards to ensure the correct flight of the javelin.

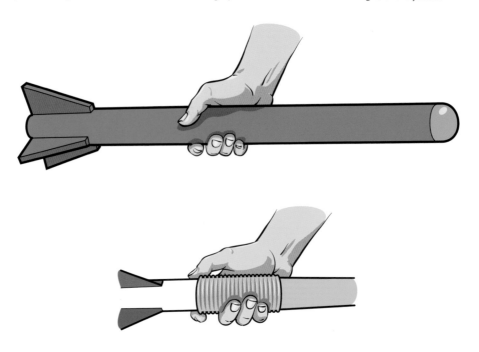

4.3.5 Javelin Progressions for the Standing Throw

The correct position of the feet and legs are key contributors to a successful throw. In the Javelin however, the most common mistake is throwing from a position that is incorrect in terms of the feet and legs. It is very important that, from an early age, young athletes are taught the correct throwing techniques. The opposite leg to the throwing arm should be placed just behind the throwing line, with the other foot placed behind about shoulder width apart. Therefore, in right-handed throwers the left foot is placed up to the line and the right foot behind. Such a position assists in making use of the powerful leg muscles. The javelin should be held in the hand with the palm facing the sky and the arm must start the throw from a straightish position to ensure maximum pull and acceleration on the javelin. The initial position will be 90% of the body weight on the right leg as the javelin is extended back and the weight is then shifted to 90% on the left leg at release.

The longer the travel of the arm before releasing, the more the path of acceleration is increased and the faster the javelin will leave the hand. The hips should be driven powerfully from right to left which leads the throwing action and adds torque velocity to the javelin. The back heel should be turned making a bow with the chest in the direction of the throw before the elbow is pulled through high with the tip of the javelin also in the direction of the throw. The young athletes can act as observers for each other and therefore have the ability to establish the angle at which the object goes furthest.

4.3.6 Javelin Progressions for the Moving Throw

After the standing throw has been mastered, the young athlete can then progress to adding further forward movement by running and then throwing. The additional speed and momentum should ensure that the implement to be thrown will go further. The young athlete should first be taught and then practise a three-stride approach before progressing to a five-stride approach. Encourage the young athlete to run at the throw, as some will run up to the line, stop and then throw. Running at the throw and not going over the throwing line is important and it must be explained to young athletes that getting their steps and actions right, even down to the final flick with the fingers and the wrist, will contribute to improvement.

4.3.6.1 The 3-Stride Approach

❶ **❷** **❸**

To begin the approach, the thrower should face the direction of the throw with both feet together and the javelin held close to the arm. In a right-handed thrower the sequence is as follows and can be seen above:

❶ The left foot should stride forward.

❷ The second stride is longer and forwards with the hips staying low onto the right foot.

❸ The emphasis of the long, fast stride will leave the body-weight back over the rear leg, taking the thrower into a strong throwing position. Just before planting the left foot the toes need to be facing slightly upwards so that the heel can contact the ground first, braking forward momentum which is then transferred to the javelin. The centre of gravity stays low and fast throughout the cross steps into the final foot plant to ensure the body is driven forwards.

Encourage young athletes to count with each stride or even to adopt a saying with an equal number of words to strides. For example, with a three-stride approach the following could be used:
'I am great' or 'I love throwing' or quickness rhythm of 1...2, 3 or A...B, C'.

4.3.6.2 The 5-Stride Approach

❶ **❷** **❸** **❹** **❺**

4.4 Discus (Sling)

The discus is a dangerous implement, so to ensure safety when coaching young athletes a soft quoit, plastic hoop or a primary discus should be used.

4.4.1 Introducing the Slinging Action

The sling can be introduced to young athletes by practising using a soft quoit or plastic hoop. Although the grip is different from that used in proper discus throwing, the young athlete can quickly and safely master the idea of 'The Slinging' action with the hips, torso and arms.

4.4.2 How to Hold the Discus

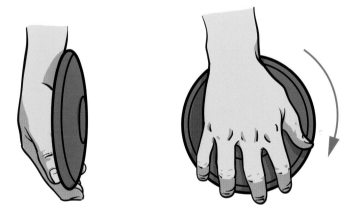

The hand does not actually hold the discus in a grip. The tips of the fingers are spread around the outer rim and the discus is actually held in place by the centrifugal force created by the swing of the arm, causing the discus to press against the fingers. Therefore, should the hand be stationary there would not be any centrifugal force and the discus would fall to the ground. Asking the young athletes to walk round in circles to get the arm to rise and hand to stay on top of the discus can assist in ensuring that the discus is held correctly.

4.4.3 Under-Arm Bowl With a Discus

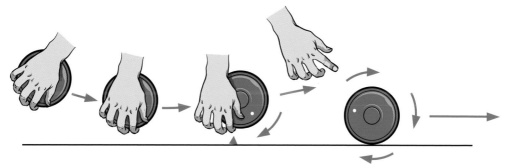

The first step that should be taught is the release of the discus using an under-arm bowl. The young athlete in the manner described in 4.4.2 holds a primary discus and should practise under-arm bowling so that the discus has forward spin from the index finger when it is projected if it is released correctly. A white dot can be painted onto the discus and when performing the practices the forward spin can be checked by the clockwise rotation of the dot. Organising the young athletes into groups of four and arranging them in a square will allow practice by rolling the discus to each other. Encourage the young athletes to keep their body low and take a small stride forwards, when rolling the discus to each other, which will allow a smooth arm swing that culminates in a full arm extension into the release position. The young athletes should attempt to roll the discus along the ground so it travels as straight as possible.

This under-arm bowling should be practised until the young athlete has obtained a reasonable amount of forward spin. This can be developed by trying the same exercise but raising the arm action little by little until the primary discus can be thrown so that it travels smoothly without wobbling. The discus is a very difficult throw as it is hard to judge when to release it and, if the implement leaves the hand wobbly, it will lose glide and therefore not travel as far.

4.4.4 Discus Progressions for a Standing Throw

View from side at start   *View from front at release*

The thrower stands at the throwing line and places the left foot at the line with the right foot set back as shown above. The heel of the right foot should be in line with the toes of the left foot to allow turning and lifting of the hips and body. The discus is held in the left hand with the palm facing upwards. The right hand is then placed over the discus with the fingers over the rim as described in 4.4.2. The throw is initiated by pivoting the feet and transferring body weight.

The discus arm is swung back with the thrower pivoting on his or her feet to the chin-knee-toe position. From here the leg action is brought into the movement to develop the fling with increased travel and momentum.

The young athlete then practises throwing the discus flat whilst obtaining the spin with the first two fingers as practised earlier with the under-arm bowling. The young athlete should be encouraged to develop confidence using a swinging motion of the throwing arm and body.

4.4.5 Discus Progressions for a Moving Throw
Young athletes under 13 years old may find it very difficult to master the concept of the full turn and accordingly the details have not been included in this manual. However, there may be an exceptional young athlete in the coaching group and therefore an intermediary stage called the South African Drill can be taught. For safety reasons this can be taught initially using plastic hoops or a tennis ball.

4.4.5.1 South African Drill

The following diagrams show the sequence in the South African Drill for right-handed throwers. It is illustrated in a throwing circle but the use of a circle is not essential for practice. The aim of the turn is to make the thrower feel the pivoting of the right foot as a direct result of the left leg drive.

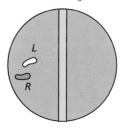

1. The starting position is with the right foot at the rear of the centre of the circle and the left foot slightly in front. The thrower should be fully wound up and facing the throwing direction.

2. The thrower then pushes off the left leg vigorously to initiate a fast right foot pivot so that the left foot is out of contact with the ground for as short a time as possible. To accomplish this the centre of gravity is kept low and orientated forwards to avoid the common error of 'leaping' across the circle.

3. When the left foot hits the ground at the front, the right foot continues to pivot and pushes the hips into a throwing action.

Young athletes should not:
- initiate the drill with the shoulders
- have the left foot land "in the bucket" (i.e. too far round to the left) at the front of the circle
- block with the left side of the body
- throw from the back foot

4.5 Hammer (Heave)

4.5.1 Introducing the Heaving Action
For safety reasons do not let young athletes throw hard or heavy hammers. However, the heave type of throw is very interesting and makes particular use of centrifugal force.

4.5.2 Practice Hammers
To facilitate the introduction of hammer throwing to young athletes, lightweight hammers have been introduced. The primary hammer comes in a variety of weights ranging from 600g–1.5kg.

The Primary Hammer

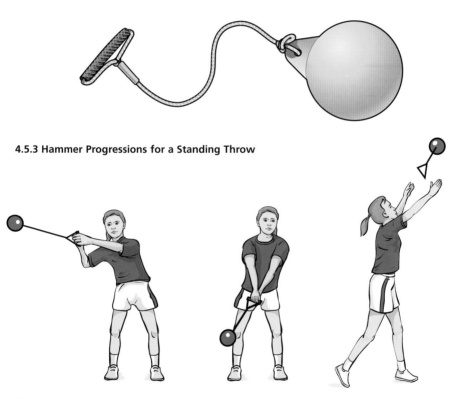

4.5.3 Hammer Progressions for a Standing Throw

When practising indoors, position the young athletes so that the hammer, when released, travels towards a wall or net and away from the group. During outdoor sessions, discipline the young athletes to stand behind the throwing line and away from the throwing area.

Let the young athletes practise using a primary hammer as shown. They should practise swinging the hammer at a slight incline over the head, which can be achieved by pulling the hands across the forehead.

The young athletes should be allowed to practise the following:

- Swinging the hammer in the correct plane
- Correct movement of the feet
- Releasing the hammer at the correct position and at the correct angle

A common fault in young athletes participating in the hammer is that of swinging the hammer in the vertical plane in front of the body or in the horizontal plane above the head. This should be discouraged at an early stage in the development of technique and can be avoided by allowing no more than two swings and then throwing on the third swing. Limiting the number of swings will also speed up the throwing time and thus allow young athletes to have more throws.

4.5.4 Hammer Progressions for a Moving Throw

After the young athletes have perfected swinging the hammer in the correct position, they can progress to trying a turn. Using a size 4 soccer ball or 1kg medicine ball, the young athletes should practise: one (first swing), two (second swing), follow the ball (first turn) and throw. They will find this relatively easy with a size 4 soccer ball or 1kg medicine ball. It is a safer way of introducing the turn than working with any kind of hammers. After several practices and when they are feeling comfortable with the turning actions, young athletes can then progress towards using a 1.5 kg plastic hammer.

4.6 Throwing Games

For good reasons, young athletes should not be throwing the real shots, javelins, discus or hammers. Competitions, however, can still be organised using quoits and soft equipment designed for both indoor and outdoor use. Young athletes can find such competitions lots of fun. In addition to throwing for distance young athletes will enjoy games that involve target throwing which will encourage them to throw for accuracy.

Again, young athletes can be involved in judging, observing and monitoring, but it is very important that young people should not be acting as judges within the throwing area when real implements are in use.

4.6.1 Bulls Eye

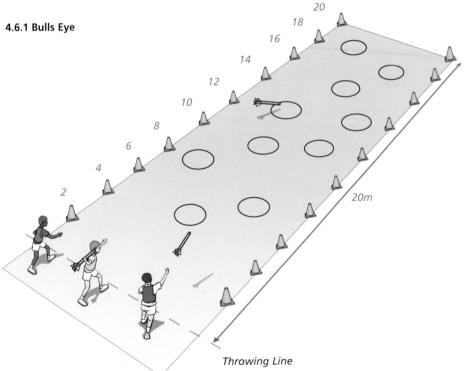

Throwing Line

Aim: Bulls Eye is a team event of throwing for accuracy and distance. The aim is for the team to score as many points as possible by throwing a specified implement (beanbag, soccer ball, soft discus, soft shot or foam javelin) as far as possible whilst trying to hit a target.

Layout: A throwing area is marked with a throwing line at one end and cones placed on the outside edges at a distance of 2 metres apart up to a distance of 20 metres. Hoops are then placed randomly inside the throwing area. Points are scored in the following way:
X points equal to the distance thrown (i.e. 12 metres = 12 points) and ten bonus points if the implement lands in a hoop.

Activity: In teams of two or three, the first young athlete from each team approaches the throwing line. The remainder of the team should stand at least 2 metres behind their thrower. The coach should instruct the young athletes that they are only allowed to 'throw' and 'collect' on his or her command. The first young athlete from the first team is then instructed to 'throw' and the coach shouts the score achieved. The first young athlete from the next team is then instructed to 'throw' and this continues until all the first team members have thrown.

All first team members are then instructed to 'collect' their implement and at this time the second team member approaches the throwing line. The above sequence continues until each team member has had three throws. The team score is calculated by totalling the points achieved by all members of the team.

4.6.2 Throws Relay

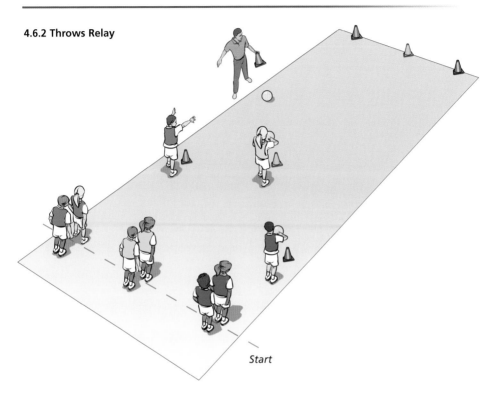

Start

Aim: The throws relay is a team event of throwing for distance a specified implement (soccer ball, primary shot or soft javelin) to reach a target using as few throws as possible.

Layout: A throwing area is marked out with a throwing line at one end and divided into lanes equal to the number of teams.

Activity: In teams of four or five, the first young athlete from each team approaches the throwing line. The remainder of the team should stand within their lane at least two metres behind their thrower. The coach should instruct the young athletes that they are only allowed to 'throw' and 'collect' on his or her command. The first young athlete from the first team is then instructed to 'throw' and the coach places a cone at the place where the implement landed. The first young athlete from the next team is then instructed to 'throw' and this continues until all the first team members have thrown.

All first team members are then instructed to 'collect' their implements and at this time the remaining members of the teams move forward in their lanes to the cone of the team nearest the initial throwing line. The second team member from each team then throws on the coach's command and the type of throw takes the same format as with the previous team member. This sequence continues until the first team reaches the target.

5.1 Introduction to Jumping

Once again, a key aspect of coaching 'jumps' sessions is the safety procedures that must be put into place. Before and during each jumps session the coach should:
- Check all equipment and landing areas are safe for use.
- Check sandpits for debris.
- Be careful not to overwork young athletes in a session.
- Be aware of other groups and their actions.
- Be watchful of throwing areas.
- Not leave equipment, such as upturned rakes, unattended.

Jumping activities can be very stressful on the young athlete's body and therefore the number of practice trials should be limited and only take place for short periods of time. All jumps have the same sequence of Approach, Take-Off, Flight and Landing and each element will contribute to the overall height or distance attained by the young athlete.

All the recognised jumping activities can fall into two different categories:
1) Vertical Jumps
2) Horizontal Jumps

5.1.1 The Skill of Jumping
Before the young athlete is introduced to specific recognised jumping actions, he or she should first be taught the skill of different types of jumps. Young athletes should learn the difference between a variety of jumping movements. The easiest way to teach this is to ask the group to perform single movement jumps as follows:

a) Hop from one foot to the same foot
    Hop forward on the left foot
    Hop forward on the right foot

b) Jump from one foot to the other foot
    Step forward from left foot to right foot
    Step forward from right foot to left foot

c) Jump from one foot to two feet
    Jump from left foot to both feet
    Jump from right foot to both feet

d) Jump from two feet to one foot
    Jump from both feet to left foot
    Jump from both feet to right foot

e) Jump from two feet to two feet

5.2 Vertical Jumps

The following jumping activities fall into the Vertical Jumps category:
Vertical Jump
High Jump
Pole Vault

5.2.1 Vertical Jump

The Vertical Jump is an internationally recognised measurement of fitness relating the ratio of leg strength to body weight and it is also an activity test that negates the advantage of height. As young athletes get fitter in terms of leg strength, their ability at this test should improve.

Young athletes can be tested using either chalk marks on a wall or an adjustable Vertical Jump Measuring Board. Initially the young athlete must stand with his or her back and head touching the wall, feet flat on the floor, and must extend both arms upwards.

A chalk mark is made at the fingertips or, if an adjustable Vertical Jump Measuring Board is used, the young athlete pushes the slider up to point as far as the fingers can reach. The full height is gained when both elbows are locked and the arms touch the side of the head.

To prepare for the jump, the young athlete dips his or her fingers into some chalk and turns sideways to the board or wall. If the young athlete is left-handed, the chalk should be on the left fingers and the left shoulder nearest the board or wall and vice-versa for right-handed young athletes. From a standing position, the young athlete bends the knees and swings the arms for lift at take-off, touching the scale at the highest point that can be reached. The measurement is taken to the nearest centimetre below the top of the chalk mark left by the strike of the young athlete's fingers.

5.2.2 High Jump

The first real technique that should be introduced to young athletes is the Scissors Jump. The main reasons for this are the fact that the Scissors Jump is a very simple activity requiring minimal specialised equipment and because it is the foundation for the most effective method of jumping, the 'Fosbury' Flop.

5.2.2.1 The Scissors Jump

Young athletes should be introduced to the Scissors Jump technique by experimenting over a low bar 30 to 40 centimetres high or even over a low plastic two-way folding hurdle. This type of hurdle is very safe and allows many groups to practise. More young athletes can be active.

It is imperative that a landing area is used and on lower heights (up to 70 centimetres) this may be a basic gymnastic mat but on fairly modest heights (greater than 70 centimetres) proper high jump landing mats should be used. If a proper high jump landing area is used, it will be beneficial to use a flexible elastic crossbar for practice purposes. However, for safety reasons ensure the uprights will not fall if the young athlete lands on this elastic crossbar. Young athletes must be allowed practice attempts from both feet before they determine which is their preferred take-off foot.

The approach for the Scissors Jump should be straight and at an approximate angle of 20–25° to the bar. This approach is more effective as there is no temptation for the young athlete to lean towards the bar, which would affect the lift at take-off.

CORNWALL COLLEGE
LEARNING CENTRE

Take-off is with the foot furthest from the bar and combined with the use of both arms drives the hips upwards. The knee of the free leg is driven up at take-off and is straightened to allow clearance over the bar. The take-off leg follows quickly so that the legs 'scissor' over the bar. Landing on low mats is with the free leg followed by the take-off leg for stability and balance. With proper high jump landing mats the young athlete can 'fall' onto the mat. The posture should be kept as upright as possible throughout the jump.

Start with a low bar and a four-stride approach with young athletes. Progress can then be made to six-stride and eight-stride approaches and to gradual increases in the height of the bar by approximately 5 centimetres at a time. It must be noted that an eight-stride approach is an optimal maximum as most young athletes cannot cope with the speed of longer approaches, which in turn will have a negative effect on their jumping ability.

5.2.2.2 The 'Fosbury' Flop

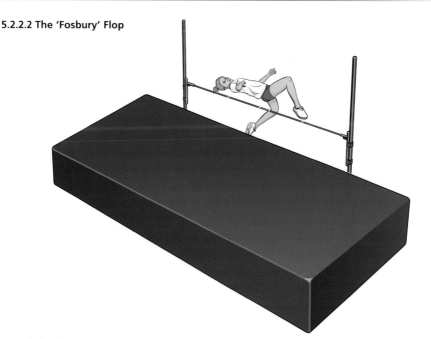

Named after its American creator, Dick Fosbury, the 'Fosbury' Flop revolutionised high jumping but it has only been possible through the introduction of modern high jump landing areas.

Competition for young athletes under 11 years is normally and quite rightly restricted to the Scissor Jump technique. The 'Scissors Jump' never needs to leave the training programme since the upright body posture is an indication of a run-through the take-off behaviour. A body that leans back in the 'Scissors Jump' will be thrown at the bar in the 'Fosbury Flop'. Since it is not uncommon for many young athletes joining Track & Field Athletic Clubs to seek to follow the elite athletes and mimic their styles, the basic technique of the 'Fosbury' Flop can be introduced in the following way:

The approach should begin straight and on the final three strides the young athletes then run on a curve. Some young athletes, however, will have a fully curved approach, but the only place the curve is required is in the final strides in preparation for take-off and the approach should gradually accelerate up to these last few strides.

Take-off is once again with foot furthest from the bar and the knee of the free leg is driven upwards towards the chest and slightly across the body introducing the rotation. It is important that the young athlete does not have his or her back to the bar before take-off. The rotation comes into effect after the young athlete has taken off and therefore the bar is crossed with the back arched down towards the mat. To complete the clearance of the bar, the head is dropped backwards, the heels will lift upwards and the young athlete lands on the mat on his or her back.

I·F·T·A

To improve the technique of arching the back when crossing the bar and the backdrop landing, the young athlete can practise the following activity. This drill is good for familiarisation and warm-up. If it is overused, however, it can introduce a 'throwing at the bar' sensation which can be detrimental to the jumping technique.

❶ Stand with the feet shoulder width apart, back to the mat and approximately 30–40 centimetres from the mat.
❷ From two feet, the arms should be driven upwards and jump up and back towards the mat.
❸ As the bar is crossed, the body should be arched and heels flicked upwards.
❹ Landing will take place on the mat with the young athlete on his or her back.
  The elastic crossbar can be raised gradually to encourage both greater drive from take-off and arching the body to ensure clearance.

❶

❷
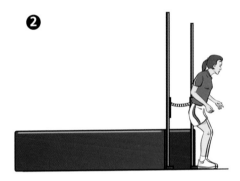

❸
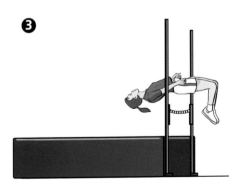

❹
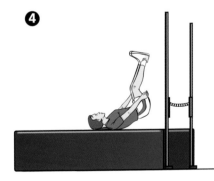

5.2.3 Pole Vault

The full pole vaulting technique is a complex skill to master both for an inexperienced coach and for the young athlete. It is possible, however, to teach the basics of how to hold, carry and swing the pole relatively easily.

5.2.3.1 How to Hold the Pole when Vaulting

Right-handed young athletes should hold the pole with the right hand at the top and the left hand approximately 45 centimetres lower down. The reverse applies for left-handers. The thumbs of both hands must be at the top and the knuckles begin by facing towards the vaulting area.

5.2.3.2 How to Carry the Pole when Running

Firstly, the young athletes should pretend they are holding a pole. If they are right-handed, their little finger on their right hand fits onto their hip or more conveniently just into a tracksuit bottom with the rest of the fingers curled and the right thumb touching the index finger. The left arm is then held at shoulder height and is bent in towards the chest with the palm away from the chest, the fingers curled and the thumb touching the index finger making a circle for the pole to go though. Once again, the reverse applies for left-handers.

When the young athletes become comfortable with this position they can then progress to practising sprinting over 20 metres with the pretend pole. Once this has been achieved a small wooden practice pole can be introduced to perform this exercise several times. The coach should be observing the technique of the young athletes and ensuring that the body does not lean forwards or backwards. If this does occur it should be rectified as soon as possible and the young athletes encouraged to be running tall with their hips high.

For safety reasons it is important that only wooden ash poles or fibreglass poles are used. Emphasise to young athletes that they should not practise at home with wooden broom shanks.

5.2.3.3 Pole Vault Practices
Crossing the Moat

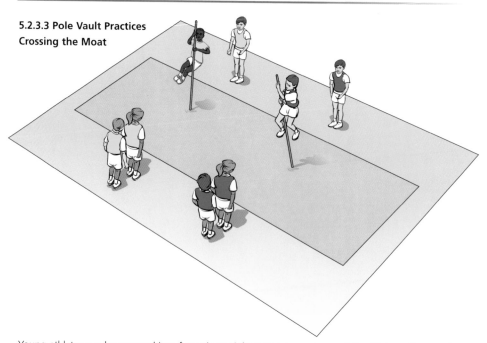

Young athletes can be grouped into four, six or eight teams around a sandpit with two, three or four teams on one side of the pit and two, three or four teams on the other side. Using small wooden poles (approximately 140–180 centimetres), the young athletes should attempt to swing to the other side and then hand the pole to the opposite team member. Right-handed vaulters will take-off with their left foot and swing on the right hand side of the pole. To encourage a more definite swing, the young athletes should be encouraged to plant their pole in the sandpit nearer to the opposite team.

As the young athletes become more proficient, they should be encouraged to take several steps before 'planting' the pole, but always ensuring other team members are situated further away. This will encourage a little speed into the vault and after a short period of time they will be clearing the width of the pit and therefore, for safety reasons, the activity should be changed to utilise the length of the pit. This activity can also be used to teach landing by progressing from striding out to striding out with a twist and twisting to land two-legged facing the launch direction.

The young athletes should now be ready to practise crossing a bar and planting their poles in a specified place. A flexible elastic crossbar can be placed across the width of the sandpit and a small box should be dug to allow for the pole plant. It is important to note that the back part of the box should be dug so it is greater than 90 degrees and therefore the young athlete is not jammed halfway through the jump. The practice should be organised such that only one athlete is attempting to vault at any one time. They must attempt to plant their pole in the box and swing over the elastic crossbar. When the young athletes are comfortable with the practice, the elastic crossbar can be raised by 5–10 centimetres at a time commencing at 25 centimetres.

5.3 Horizontal Jumps

The following recognised jumping activities fall into the Horizontal Jumps category:
Standing Long Jump
Long Jump
Standing Triple Jump
Triple Jump

5.3.1 Standing Long Jump

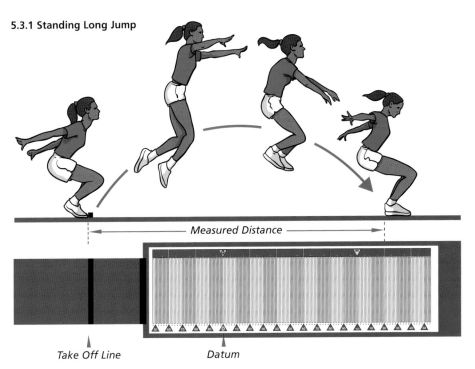

The Standing Long Jump is quite a straightforward event that young athletes will quickly master. However, they should not be 'trained' specifically for this event but encouraged by simple advice how to improve their performance. The event is beneficial both to the young athlete and to the coach as it involves the development of co-ordination and leg strength, which are good indicators of level of fitness.

The Standing Long Jump requires a two footed take-off from behind the take-off line. If practising outdoors, the Standing Long Jump can be performed into a sandpit or for indoor purposes a graduated landing mat may be used for ease of measuring. The athlete starts with feet hip-width apart and swinging the arms. Techniques involving a 'crouch' or 'rock' leading up to the jump should be encouraged provided both feet remain alongside each other and in contact with the ground/mat from the start of the action to the actual commencement of the jump. On commencement of the jump, the young athlete should swing the arms powerfully forwards and upwards, which will assist the thrust of the legs and body.

The arms swing back just before landing adding body-leg distance and then swing forwards as part of the 'soft' landing to assist in forward rotation. Landing in the Standing Long Jump should be on two feet and kept 'soft' with plenty of 'give' in the knees. It does not need to be a dead stop, as the young athlete can step forward after the jump but any step back or touching the mat behind the feet with any part of the body counts as a 'no jump'. Therefore, it may be advantageous for the young athlete to rotate forwards on landing.

5.3.2 Long Jump

All jumping activities including the Long Jump can be broken down into several phases:
1) The Approach
2) The Take-Off
3) The Flight
4) The Landing

Ultimately only the speed of the approach and the lift at take-off can determine the distance jumped, however, efficiency can be improved with the flight and landing techniques used. For the purposes of coaching young athletes in the long jump technique, the take-off and flight are the first skills that are practised, followed by the landing and finally the approach skill. Consistency can then be mastered.

5.3.2.1 The Take-Off

The lift at take-off and the posture in flight are very important to the success of the jump and with minor adjustments can significantly increase the distance jumped. The technique at take-off should be as follows:

1. The free leg is swung through quickly with the knees flexed high and the following heel kept up until the athlete has taken off.
2. The action of the arms at take-off is one of lifting and continuing of the running action to ensure forward momentum.
3. The jumping leg should strike backwards and downwards to give lift. Full hip and leg extension should be sought in the split-second it takes to execute take-off.

The diagram illustrates two effective drills:

1 The young athlete strides out over a two-way plastice hurdle to feel the sensation of jumping for height as well as distance.

2 A 'Jump Aid' is held out by the coach and the young athlete tries to touch it to feel the sensation of reach and tall posture during flight.

5.3.2.2 The Flight

The next practice for the young athletes should be the flight phase movement from a one-footed take-off with the other leg able to swing free. The sequence of learning can progress from short approach 'pops' and landing in a lunge position to in-air walking landing in a lunge on the other leg. The idea is to keep a good full stride in the air and to avoid 'foot flutter' during the jump. Once this has been mastered, progress can then be made to four-stride, six-stride and eight-stride approaches.

The 'in flight' action illustrated in the diagram shows the legs being swung forward through the flight and towards the landing. This action is counter-balanced by swinging the arms forward above the head. The landing pose, if started too early, results in forward rotation of the body so that the young athlete pitches forwards at landing. Therefore, keeping the body as long as possible in the air for as great a period of time as possible delays the rotation.

5.3.2.3 The Landing

The landing is executed as an outgrowth of the hitch (or hang) just before landing, with the arms balancing the move then swinging back just before touchdown. The legs should be kept as high as possible for as long as possible and the arms pushed backwards to increase the lift of the legs. The arms sweep forwards as the heels contact and the knees 'give' so that the young athlete does not fall back. The young athletes should be encouraged to keep the landing as 'soft' as possible by ensuring they have plenty of 'give' in the knees. The aim is to land with both heels in line as the measurement is taken from the point made by the young athlete that is closest to the board.

5.3.2.4 The Approach

Acceleration   *Preparation Attack*

After the young athletes have practised the take-off, flight and landing into the pit from a short four, six and eight-stride approach, a full approach can now be considered. For young athletes this will normally be in the range from ten strides to sixteen strides. Longer approaches will serve no purpose as optimum speed can be reached in this distance. Each young athlete's individual ability must be taken into account when deciding the number of strides for the approach. Those with less sprinting fitness should be encouraged to use a shorter approach. To ensure accuracy on a regular basis the start of any approach must be from a stationary position.

A ten-stride to sixteen-stride approach is roughly divided into three sections:
• Acceleration
• Preparation
• Attack

An observer counts the steps of the young athlete who runs from the take-off board back along the runway in a similar manner to that of the normal approach when jumping. The position of the foot on the fourteenth stride is noted by the observer who places a personal marker in that place alongside the runway. Fine adjustments to this marker position can then be made.

The observer standing by the take-off board will tell the athlete if the take-off foot is landing short or over the board. Adjustments can be made to the marker position until the athlete achieves take-off exactly on the board. Obviously as the athlete becomes more proficient, by improving the run-up and style of attack, further adjustments will be required. Indeed, slight alterations will probably be required on each occasion to compensate for wind, weather and track surface.

5.3.3 Co-ordination Exercises
Co-ordination is a vital factor in the success of young athletes in all events and especially so in such events as the triple jump and hurdles. Co-ordination exercises can be used as introductory activities to these events and examples are detailed on the following pages:

5.3.3.1 Star Jumps

The young athlete should start by standing with both feet together and in one movement perform a 'Star' Jump, which is basically a matter of stretching arms and legs in mid-air before landing with both feet together.

5.3.3.2 Kick Jumps

The young athlete should start by standing with both feet together and in one movement perform a 'Kick' Jump, which is basically a matter of kicking one foot forward and one foot backwards in mid-air before landing with both feet together. The exercise is repeated by kicking of the opposite foot forward.

5.3.3.3 Bunny-Hop Jumps

Bunny-Hops, which are two-footed jumps, can be introduced by gradually progressing from one Bunny-Hop to two Bunny-Hops to three Bunny-Hops and so on up to approximately seven Bunny-Hops. The young athletes should be encouraged to adopt a rhythm to ensure they proceed smoothly. Small two-way plastic folding hurdles can be introduced for the young athletes to Bunny-Hop over, which is a very basic form of plyometric training.

5.3.3.4 Combination Jumps

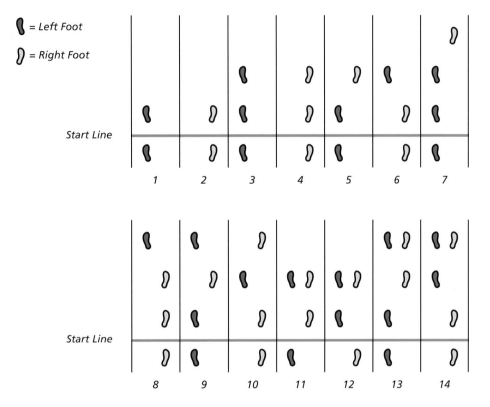

Combination jumps will assist with improving the co-ordination of a young athlete and can be introduced in the following way. For safety reasons and to avoid collisions it is important the young athletes all work in the same direction and from a level starting position.

It is possible to devise a more complex series of 'combinations', which can be a lot of fun. Young athletes can be asked to practise in their own time to improve performance for the next session. The coach and the young athlete can be very imaginative and innovative in the way they create new combinations, but safety should always be kept in mind.

5.3.4 Standing Triple Jump

The description 'Triple Jump' can be rather bewildering to a young athlete so it can be simplified to the description of 'Hop, Step and Jump', which can be practised in the combination jumps described in section 5.3.3.4.

5.3.4.1 Introducing the Three Phases

For the Standing Triple Jump, both the of athlete's feet must be behind the start line but they need not be together. The young athlete may crouch or rock before the jump but the leading front foot must not break contact with the ground before the start of the jump. This rule does not apply to the back foot which may be swung freely provided it does not touch the ground in front of the start line. The measurement is taken from the take-off line to the nearest point of impression in the sand pit measured at 90° to the take-off line.

Most young athletes will not be able to get the sequence right away but it can be a lot of fun learning and there can be quite a sense of achievement when it is mastered. The event involves thinking and co-ordination. It can be done into a sand pit or by using a graduated Triple Jump Landing Mat.

Many young athletes have a particular problem with the starting hop. If young athletes are having difficulty, they can be advised to hold the free foot on take-off. As they land, before trying the step, they should let go of the free foot and drive forwards with the knee. This will assist them in mastering the hop and step phases.

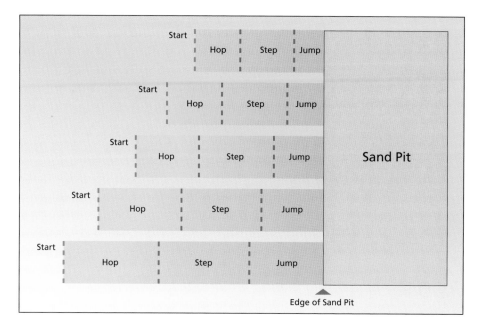

A triple jump grid can be set up at the side of a sandpit providing the ground is safe. The young athletes should begin triple jumping from the start line nearest the sandpit and progress along the start lines until they find the one that most suits their jumping ability. This kind of grid can also aid the coach in observing where the weaknesses (if any) are in the young athlete's jump.

5.3.5 Running Triple Jump (six metres limited approach)

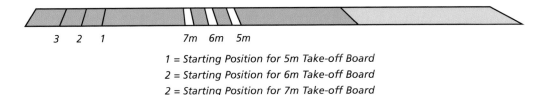

3   2   1   7m   6m   5m

1 = Starting Position for 5m Take-off Board
2 = Starting Position for 6m Take-off Board
2 = Starting Position for 7m Take-off Board

This is intended as an intermediate stage for young athletes over the age of 11 years progressing from the Standing Triple Jump to the formal triple jump. The six metres limited approach should be strictly applied and is necessary to prevent the young athletes building up excessive speed when approaching the take-off board.

Take-off lines can be chalked on the approach at distances of five metres, six metres and seven metres from the beginning of the sand pit and cones placed at 11, 12 and 13 metres to denote the respective six metres limited approaches.

A young athlete aged 11–13 years will normally take approximately four or five strides in the six metres approach and therefore, in a similar method to that used in the Long Jump, a run-up should be marked out.

The young athlete must try to establish a technique whereby the landings and take-offs are flat-footed to provide stability and avoid ankle injuries. A sound rhythm will aid the distance jumped and the following ratio should be sought:

Hop - 37%	Step - 30%	Jump - 33%

To the young athlete the hop 'feels' flat and fast, although the distance covered is more. With each landing and take-off some horizontal or forward momentum is lost and so the step and jump phases 'feel' longer and higher. If the hop 'feels' long and high they are likely either to be jumping high and landing with a straight leg or the approach is too fast for them to handle at that time. It is very important to limit the number of practices by a young athlete, as the Triple Jump is an activity that has a very high impact on the joints of a growing body.

5.4 Jumping Games

Team games and challenges can be organised, both indoor and outdoor, that are related to the main content of the jumping activity session. Teams can be selected so that the stronger members can encourage and work with the weaker members of the group and, therefore, no young athlete is singled out for his or her jumping ability.

5.4.1 Kangaroo Time

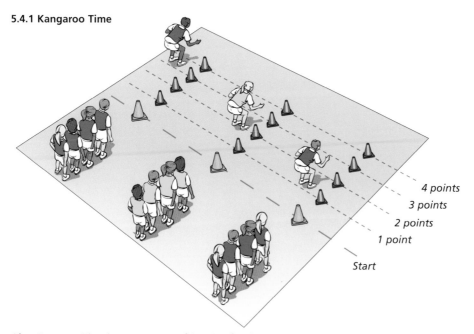

Aim: Kangaroo Time is a team event of jumping for distance, to score points in a specified manner (Standing Long Jump, Standing Triple Jump or Combination Jumps).

Equipment: Gym Mats, if performing the activity indoor
Grassed area (not wet), if performing the activity outdoors
Cones to define point lines

Layout: Jumping grids are marked with lines at one, two, three and four points for each team. The grids should be set such that every young athlete can achieve the 1 point line and at least one member of the group can achieve the 4 point line.

Activity: Each team is allocated a jumping grid and in teams of five or six, the first young athlete from each team approaches the jumping line. The remainder of the team should stand within their grid at least 2 metres behind their jumper . The first young athlete from each of the teams is then instructed to 'jump' and points awarded dependent upon which line the heel of the foot cleared. The next team member then completes a jump in the same manner. This continues until the team has completed twenty jumps. The winning team is the one with the highest point score.

5.4.2 Jumps Relay

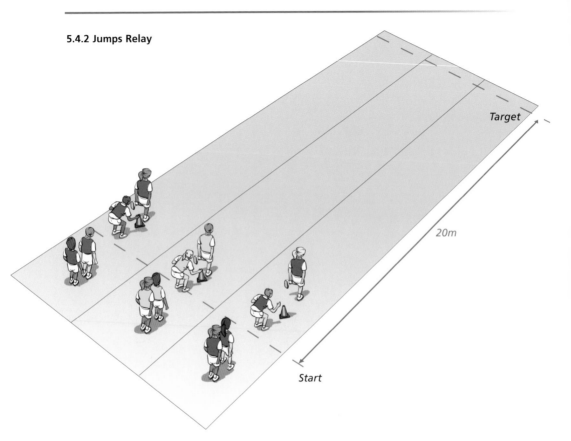

Target

20m

Start

Aim: The jumps relay is a team event of jumping for distance in a specified way (Hop, Standing Long Jump, Standing Triple Jump etc.) to reach a target with as few jumps as possible.

Equipment: Gym Mats, if performing the activity indoor
Grassed area (not wet), if performing outdoors
Cones to define jumping area and act as markers

Layout: A jumping area is marked out with a starting line at one end and is divided into lanes equal to the number of teams.

Activity: In teams of four or five, the first young athlete from each team approaches the jumping line. The remainder of the team should stand within their lane at least 2 metres behind their jumper . The first young athlete from each of the teams is then instructed to 'jump' and a cone is placed at the heel of where he or she landed. The second team member of each team, when instructed, now performs a jump from the team cone and the cone is moved to the heel of where he or she landed. This sequence continues until the first team reaches the target.

5.4.3 'Boing'

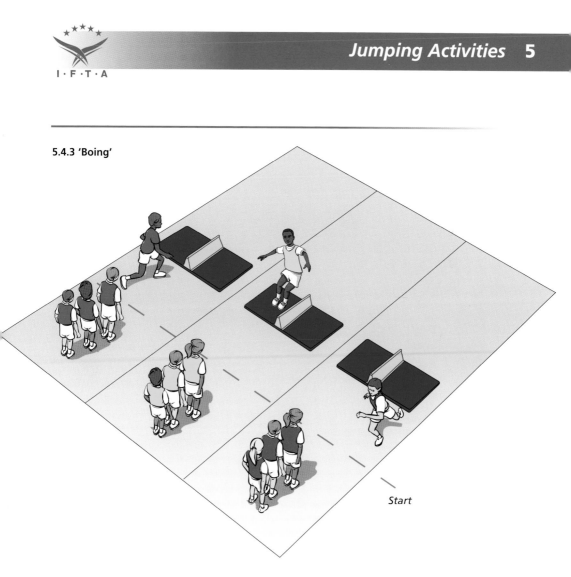

Start

Aim: Boing is a team relay event of speed bouncing. Each team must try to gain as many points as possible in a specified time period.

Equipment: Speed Bounce Mats (one per team)

Layout: A lane is marked for each team with a starting line and a speed bounce mat is placed 2 metres in front of the line.

Activity: The first team member of each team approaches the start line with the remainder of the team in a straight line behind. On the start whistle, the first team member runs towards the speed bounce mat, completes ten Speed Bounce and runs off the mat and around the lane to join the back of the team, ensuring that the next team member is not obstructed. As soon as the first team member leaves the mat, the second team member should set off and complete his or her ten Speed Bounces. This continues until all members of the team have had a turn.

5.4.4 Jumps Circuit

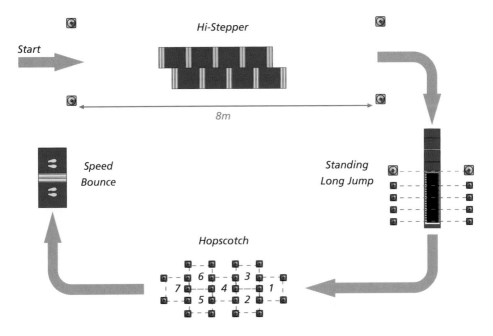

Aim: The Jumps Circuit is a team event and it involves a variety of jumping and speed activities. Members of the team must try to score as many points as possible by performing as many of the specified jumps as they can within a set time period.

Equipment: Speed Bounce Mats
Hi-Stepper
Mats for Standing Long Jump
Cones or chalk for marking Hopscotch

Layout: Each piece of equipment should be placed in the area to form a square, ensuring that there is adequate space for the whole team to congregate around the equipment. The Hi-Stepper is set up with cones 8 metres apart and the equipment placed in the centre of the cones. A Standing Long Jump grid is set up as in the game of Kangaroo Time. A Hopscotch grid is marked with cones and the coach can determine the exact layout.

Activity: The group should be split into four teams and each team situated next to a specific piece of equipment. Points are scored in the following way:

- Hi-Stepper–a return trip gains 1 point and each member of the team must complete the return run before the next member can go.

- Standing Long Jump. Points are awarded for the line cleared and the rules are the same as the game of Kangaroo Time.

- Hopscotch–a return trip gains 1 point and each member must complete the return run before the next member can go.

- Speed Bounce 10 Speed Bounce = 1 point and the rules are the same as for the game Boing.

Each activity will last between one and two minutes depending upon the number in each team. The members must try and score as many points as possible on each piece of activity. A small rest period should be given as the teams rotate around the circuit. The team with the highest points after performing on each piece of equipment will be the winners.

I·F·T·A

6.1 Introduction to Speed

Speed in running terms is determined by:

Frequency of Stride x Length of Stride

Therefore, to improve a young athlete's personal best times over specified distances, at least one of the above must be increased and married technically to the other. Running activities that are known as speed events in track and field athletics include all individual sprinting distances up to 400 metres, all relays up to 4 x 400 metres and all hurdle events.

6.2 Sprinting & Sprinting Drills

6.2.1 Sprinting Technique

When running, at any speed, the legs are used to carry and push the bodyweight forward. The push is achieved through the contact of the feet with the ground, which should be relatively quiet. If a loud heavy-footed noise comes from young athletes' feet when they run, it should be pointed out. It is surprising that when a young athlete strives to get rid of the noise, he or she will quickly develop correct foot action.

A good running technique results in economic use of energy, but the technique differs between sprinters and distance runners. Basically, the assistance of the arm drive backwards is important to the sprinter whilst for the distance runner the emphasis of the arms is on balance. The sprinter will also run on the balls of his or her feet to create the push whilst the distance runner uses the whole of the foot. The knee lift in a sprinter is also much higher as this potentially increases stride length.

The drive of the arm backwards will counter-balance the action of the opposite leg, such that the left arm balances the right leg and the right arm balances the left leg. The arms must not be swung from side to side as it encourages body twisting which will be counter-balanced by the leg action and thus the technique will become inefficient and will waste energy. Core stability is very important as the arms and legs work off the torso and midriff. A young athlete should be encouraged to opt for considerable arm travel, which will start like the pulling of a bell rope before the arm opens out to travel backwards. If the arm action is cut short when sprinting this will also cut the leg action short. It is important that the young athlete remains relaxed throughout the sprinting action and therefore the hands should be held loosely. Many young athletes will have different techniques when trying to achieve an efficient sprinting action and the coach must remember to treat each young athlete as an individual.

The coach stands in a position so that they can observe the young athlete running towards them. The coach will note that some young athletes will run quite smoothly whilst others will wobble and twist which should raise questions about the efficiency and correctness of their leg action.

Getting young athletes to hold a baton in both hands across their stomach keeping their elbows tucked in, which will not allow them to use their arms, and running as fast as possible can check for correct leg action.

During sprinting practices the coach should look for:
- good posture - tall yet relaxed
- head focussing straight forward - 10–20m ahead
- driving arm action and considerable arm travel - from the shoulders
- high knee lift in a cycling type action - foot climbs over calf
- powerful leg drive and heel lift in follow through - pull and push

6.2.2 Sprinting Drills
The following drills are not included to imitate proper sprint form but to exaggerate movements and actions found within an effective sprinting technique, thus allowing the young athlete to apply these movements and actions to increase efficiency and speed. A selection of the following drills should be performed in training shoes as part of the warm-up routine over a distance of approximately 20–25 metres and no more than one or two times each.

6.2.2.1 Walking Tall

Purpose: To strengthen muscles in lower leg and develop balance.

Action: The young athlete should walk on the balls of the feet and ensure the heels do not come into contact with the ground. The free leg is raised to a point so that the thigh is parallel with the ground and the leg action is alternated every step.

6.2.2.2 Cross Stitch

Purpose: To improve co-ordination and increase flexibility in the hips.

Action: The young athlete should perform this drill on the balls of the feet, sideways and at a fairly quick jogging pace. The arms should be extended to the side to limit the rotation of the upper body. The following sequence should then be performed:
1) Right leg is driven across the front of the left leg
2) Left leg is driven to be opposite the right leg at a distance of approximately shoulder width apart
3) Right leg is then driven across the back of the left leg
4) Left leg is driven to be opposite the right leg at a distance of approximately shoulder width apart
5) Sequence repeated for the 20–25 metres distance and the drill is then repeated with their left leg leading the drive in front and behind the right leg.

The above activity can be varied by:
1) Repeated cross-steps in front of the body without the cross-steps behind the body.
2) Arms held out straight in such a way that the body takes the form of a 'T' position.

I·F·T·A

6.2.2.3 High Skips or Leaps

Purpose: To develop rear foot and leg drive.

Action: The young athlete should perform this drill on the balls of the feet. The rear leg should drive so that the body is lifted off the ground with the assistance of the drive backwards of the opposite arm. Their free leg is raised to a point so that the thigh is parallel with the ground and the leg performing the drive is alternated every step.

6.2.2.4 Back Flicks

Purpose: To develop correct leg action (thigh high, heel high and toe up) following a drive off the rear leg.

Action: The young athlete should perform this drill on the balls of the feet, keeping the arms driving throughout and at high speed. Their knee is driven upwards, the heel flicked backwards towards the buttocks and the thigh raised to a high position.

6.2.2.5 Hi-Stepper

8m

Purpose: To develop agility, co-ordination and speed with the emphasis on bringing the thigh to a point at which it is parallel to the ground.

Action: The Hi-Stepper drill takes place over a distance of approximately 8 metres, which includes a small approach run and small run off. The young athlete should perform this drill on the balls of the feet, keeping the arms driving throughout and at high speed. The knees are raised to a point such that the feet clear the foam obstacles and are driven at speed back to the floor. Each wedge should be cleared in turn so that the young athlete will have performed five high and fast steps on each leg.

Equipment: An IFTA approved Hi-Stepper which consists of ten soft foam wedges that attach to a non-slip basemat by velcro.

6.2.2.6 Relax and Drive

Purpose: To develop relaxation in the hands, wrists and arms when running at speed.

Action: The young athlete should place a potato chip between the index finger and the thumb of each hand. He or she should then try to sprint without crushing the potato chips. This drill should be performed in pairs, as the young athletes will then be able to imitate race pressure, which can cause tension throughout the body.

6.3 Sprinting Practices

6.3.1 Standing Starts

① On the command 'on your marks' the young athlete approaches the start line and places one foot just behind the line with the other foot approximately 50 centimetres behind with both feet facing straight forward. It is usual that the front leg will be the strongest leg. The arms should be relaxed at the side of the body.

② On the command 'set', the young athlete bends both knees, places the weight over the front leg and rises to the ball of the back foot. The opposite arm to the front leg is then held forwards ready to drive backwards on 'go'. The opposite hand may be placed on the front thigh above the knee to aid balance.

③ On the command 'go' the young athlete must drive the front arm backwards and the back leg forwards, driving the foot to the ground as quickly as possible. The group can now observe each other at the start and they should notice that there is either a pause whilst the body weight is moved forward or, more likely, the young athlete takes a slight step back with the front foot. These actions take approximately half a second, which is potentially a loss of 3 metres in distance.

6.3.2 Crouch Starts

On the command 'on your marks' the young athlete approaches the start line and measures for a crouch start. A very simple way for a young athlete to measure the distance from the start line for a crouch start is as follows, assuming the left leg is the stronger:

- Kneel with both knees at the start line
- Move the knee of the right leg in line with the toe of the left leg
- Lift the left knee off the ground; left foot, right knee and right foot all remain in contact with the ground
- Place hands behind start line, with fingers pointing outwards and thumbs pointing inwards about shoulder width apart

However, there is a more accurate way of measuring the distance from the start line for a crouch start that can be taught to young athletes as they progress. The measurement is performed in the following way, assuming the left leg is the stronger:

1) place the left foot to the line
2) the right foot is then placed behind the heel of the left foot to make an 'L' shape
3) the left foot is then placed behind the heel of the right foot
4) the right foot is then placed approximately 50 centimetres behind the left foot, a small distance apart, with both feet facing straight forward
5) both knees are then bent with the knee of the right leg touching the ground directly opposite the toes of the left foot and about a fist width apart
6) the hands are then placed behind the start line, slightly more than shoulder width apart
7) the fingers point outwards and the thumb inwards to form a bridge to complete the 'on your marks' position.

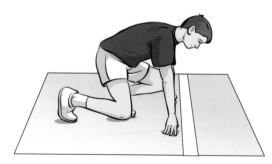

On the command 'set' the buttocks are raised slowly to a position slightly higher than the shoulders. It is important that the young athlete has his or her weight in front of the legs to facilitate a powerful push on the 'go' command.

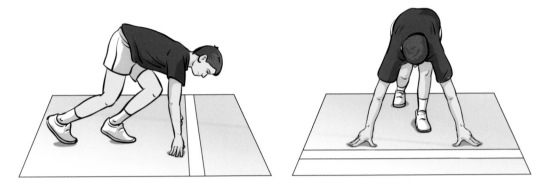

On the command 'go' the young athlete drives the body forward with the quick movement of the legs and arms. It is important to remain low out of the start and the body is gradually raised into the full sprinting technique after a distance of approximately 20–30 metres.

Some young athletes will find it difficult to understand why the feet are placed so far behind the line in a crouch start as it appears to be giving distance away. It is important therefore, to highlight that by appearing to sacrifice half a metre in a crouch start position, they can gain approximately 3 metres more in distance than if they were using a standing start.

6.3.3 Starting Practices

6.3.3.1 The Standing Up Test

It is very important that the young athletes get away at the start of the 'bang' and not the end of the 'bang'. To illustrate this to the young athletes there is a very simple practice that can be performed.

The proper initial starting procedures are carried out for a sprint start:
'on your marks'
'set'
but instead of the 'go' command 'stand up' is shouted.

Some of the young athletes will start as they would in a proper race and some will stand up. Those who stood up had listened to the complete command before they responded because, had they started at the beginning of the command, they would have been moving forward before hearing exactly what was shouted.

6.3.3.2 The Noise Test

The young athletes should be organised in one group in a line. They are instructed that on the 'on your marks' command they crouch with their backs to the line and on the 'go' command they quickly stand up. At some stage another adult should then, without the knowledge of the group, shout 'away' instead of the coach shouting 'go'. Some young athletes will still stand up whilst others will look puzzled. It should be explained to the group that they should respond to the start of any loud noise – not just to the noise made by the starter.

6.3.3.3 Reaction Tests

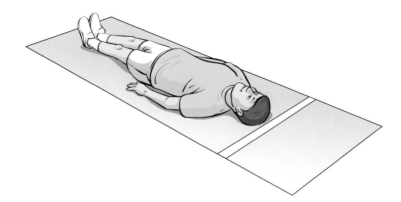

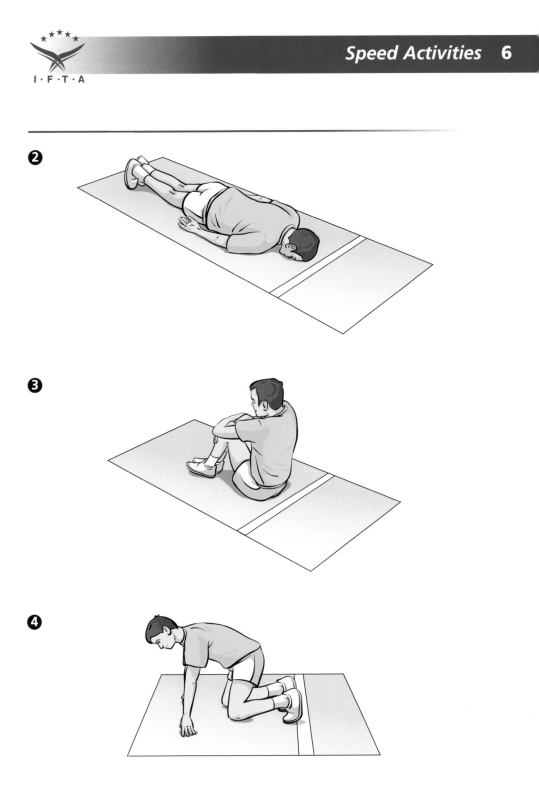

⑤

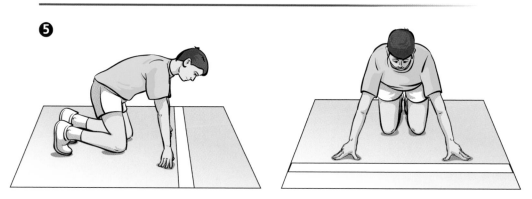

The young athletes should be organised in groups of four or five, to perform a series of reaction tests. When the 'on your marks' command is given the young athlete adopts one of the following starting positions as instructed by the coach:

❶ Lying on back   -   head near start line
❷ Lying on front   -   head near start line
❸ Sat down holding knees   -   back to start line
❹ Box position   -   back to start line
❺ Box position   -   head near start line

On the 'go' command, the young athletes must get up from the specified position and run as fast as they can a distance of approximately 10–20 metres. For all of the tests, the coach should be positioned in front and to one side of the start line to shout the commands.

6.3.3.4 Understanding the Starter
Understanding the role and responsibilities of the starter is an important consideration for a sprinter. The starter calls the young athletes to their marks on the command 'on your marks'. At this stage the Starter's Assistant quickly checks that the young athletes are in the correct position with their fingers and toes behind the starting line. All the young athletes must be stationary before the starter will give the next command 'set'. Again the starter will wait for all the young athletes to be stationary before firing the gun. If there is any fidgeting in either the 'on your marks' or 'set' positions, the starter may ask the young athletes to stand up before beginning the starting procedure again.

6.3.3.5 10m Championships

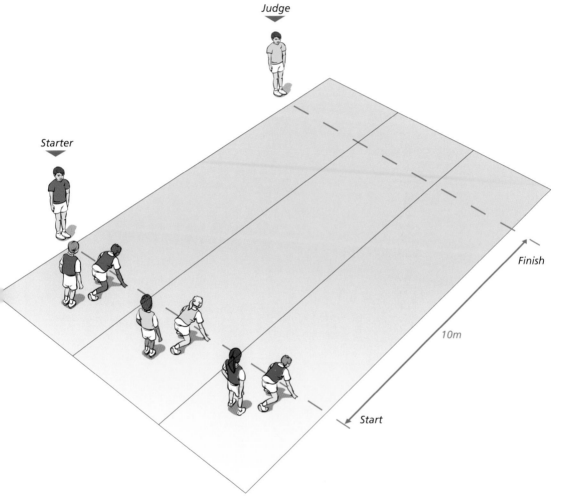

The young athletes should work in pairs and one becomes an observer whilst the other performs the activity. The observer should check that the legs, feet and hands are in the right place for the correct starting position. Young athletes can also be used as starters and judges if required and the roles of observer and performer should be changed after each turn.

6.4 Introduction to Hurdling

There are several key safety factors that must be adhered to when carrying out hurdles sessions, which are as follows:
- Ensure young athletes never cross the hurdle in the wrong direction when using proper track hurdles.
- Ensure that weights (if applicable) are set for the correct toppling resistance.
- Never have young athletes hurdling on wet grass.
- Ensure all equipment is in good repair and safe to use (no splinters in the hurdle tops etc.).

It is very important to emphasise to young athletes at the very beginning that hurdling is not a jumping activity. If a young athlete runs and jumps over the hurdles the centre of gravity has to be lifted at each hurdle and this takes a lot of effort and will slow the young athlete down. Therefore, if the young athlete can develop a method of going over the hurdles by minimising the lift of his or her centre of gravity it will save energy and should be much quicker. Young athletes should be encouraged to 'run over the hurdles' rather than 'jump over the hurdles'.

6.5 Hurdling & Hurdle Drills

6.5.1 Hurdle Rhythm
6.5.1.1 Stage One

◯ Right Foot Over   ◯ Left Foot Over

The young athlete should first be introduced to hurdling by practising running over markers with both legs. This can be achieved by allowing the young athlete to run over the markers to encourage cyclic tall running and rhythm. Markers should be placed approximately one metre apart and ideally should alternate between two different colours. The young athlete starts at the first blue marker leading with the right foot and then steps over the red marker with the left foot and continues to the end of the line of cones.

6.5.1.2 Stage Two

The markers should now be moved so they are approximately two metres apart and two lanes should be set up. The young athlete runs over the blue markers with the right leg leading, saying 'down one' over each one and returns over the red markers with the left leg leading, again saying 'down one' over each one. This will encourage a good and appropriate rhythm.

6.5.1.3 Stage Three

The markers should be placed approximately four metres apart and the young athlete runs over the blue markers with the right leg leading he or she takes three strides between them saying 'down, one, two, three' and returns over the red markers with the left leg leading in exactly the same manner.

6.5.1.4 Stage Four

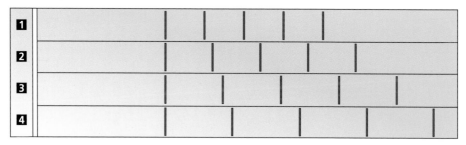

The above diagram illustrates a typical layout for a hurdles grid. The young athletes should start in lane one and progress along the lanes until they find a lane in which they are comfortable with a three-stride rhythm having tried each leg acting as the 'lead' leg.

6.5.2 The 'Lead' Leg

When the young athletes have chosen which 'lead' leg they prefer and their confidence has grown, small two-way plastic folding hurdles can be introduced in place of the markers. The height of these should be gradually increased from 10 centimetres to 20 centimetres through to 50 centimetres.

Start in centre of hurdle line

Only lead leg going over hurdle

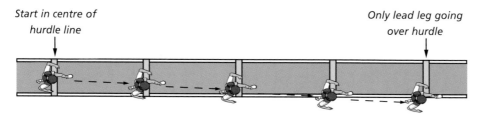

As the height of the hurdle increases to 30 centimetres or more, the young athlete can now start to perform 'lead' leg drills. These are initially carried out by the young athlete running over the middle of the first hurdle and gradually moving a little further to one side so that by the last two or three hurdles of a line of six or seven, only the 'lead' leg is actually going over the hurdle. The drill is performed in this manner as no technique has been acquired with the 'other' leg and the centre of gravity would automatically be lifted too much over each hurdle. This drill is performed so that the young athlete can focus on posture and speed without worrying about the 'trail' leg actions.

Performing the drill over the side of the hurdle will enable the young athlete to focus on the 'lead' leg technique and the emphasis should always be on the speed of the action.

As the height of the hurdle increases, in order to maintain efficiency over the hurdles the following technique will need to be adopted:

(a) fast bent knee lift at hurdle

(b) driving straight forward with toe up

(c) hook lead leg heel over hurdle, like a coat-hanger onto a rail

(d) fast leg down once over the hurdle

6.5.3 The 'Trail' Leg

Once the 'lead' leg has been mastered the 'other leg', which is known as the 'trail' leg can be practised. The young athlete should go to the other side of the hurdle so that only the 'trail' leg will actually go over the hurdle.

Assuming in the illustration that the left leg is the 'lead' leg and therefore the right leg will be the 'trail' leg, the young athlete should walk towards the first hurdle. When he or she are approximately 70 centimetres from the hurdle, a chalk or tape mark should be placed on the track.

The young athlete should now take a long step forward so that the left foot is placed just in front of the upright of the hurdle. The placement of the foot is extremely important and directly relates to correct technique when later attempting to jog or run over a hurdle with only the 'trail' leg performing the action. As the long step is taken, the arms are used to maintain balance by swinging the opposite arm forward and then pulling back to recover. The 'trail' leg recovers to a high knee position so that the young athlete maintains a sprint action.

The drill is initially performed by the young athlete walking over one side of the first two hurdles so that only the 'trail' leg is actually going over the hurdle. He or she can then gradually speed up a little so that by the last two or three hurdles of a line of six or seven the activity is carried out at speed. The trail leg action can also be developed as follows:

1) walk over hurdles with three high knee steps between each hurdle

2) run over hurdles with three high knee steps between each hurdle

Move hurdles closer together and;

3) walk over hurdles with one high knee step between each hurdle

4) run over hurdles with one high knee step between each hurdle

Once again, as the height of the hurdle increases, in order to maintain efficiency over the hurdles the following technique will need to be adopted:
(a) Trail leg is pulled around and forwards with ankle tucked in and toes rotated up.
(b) Trail leg continues round and forwards into a high knee sprint action.
(c) The young athlete continues with a driving sprint action.

After isolating specific elements of the hurdle technique to correct faults and improve technique, the young athlete can then perform the activity as a whole action over the middle of the hurdle. However, mixing centre / lead / trail leg drills reinforces effective hurdle sprinting. Hurdling is primarily a sprinting event so development of quick action and leg speed is essential.

6.6 Introduction to Relays

Most young athletes will have probably performed a stationary take-over in the form of linear shuttle relays, which have little in common with what needs to be achieved within a proper relay take-over. Initial practice in coaching sessions should therefore involve going back to basics and highlighting the benefits of using a moving take-over.

The baton should not stop at any take-over point, as it is essential that it keeps moving forward at speed to minimise the time taken to exchange. To achieve this forward movement at speed, when the exchange takes place the outgoing runner needs to be running as quickly as the incoming runner. Therefore, the outgoing runner must start running before the incoming runner.

Ideally, if the outgoing runner manages to keep just ahead of the incoming runner at the time of the take-over then some distance can be gained by the arms in passing the baton forward. Timing the take-over is very important. An outgoing runner who sets off too soon will either have to stop to receive the baton or the incoming runner will not reach him or her. If the outgoing runner sets off too late, he or she may be overtaken by the incoming runner and the baton.

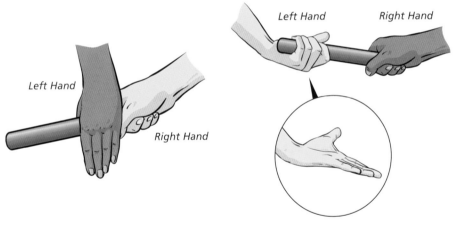

Upsweep Pass   *Downsweep Pass*

For young athletes aged 8–13 years, a good introduction to relays is by the 'upsweep' method, which is an upward swing into the downward facing 'V' of the outgoing runner's hand. This is the safest method of exchanging the baton. The 'downsweep' technique is not preferred for use with young athletes as this requires many hours of practice and a lot of competition experience to master technique and timing. The essential skill to be developed at take-over is that of ensuring the baton remains moving forward at speed.

The 10 metres acceleration zone before the take-over box should not be used with young athletes as far too often they are disqualified for exchanging before the box. This was introduced for senior international sprinters and the 20 metres of the take-over box is ample distance for young athletes.

The traditional method of baton exchange for a 4 x 50 metres or 4 x 100 metres relay team is as follows:

1st Runner	-	starts and runs with baton in right hand
2nd Runner	-	takes and runs with baton in left hand
3rd Runner	-	takes and runs with baton in right hand
4th Runner	-	takes and runs with baton in left hand

This sequence is the preferred sequence for the 4 x 100 metres relay teams so that the young athletes who will be running on the bends (1st runner and 3rd runner) are on the inside of the lane at take-over and they can continue to run close to the inside line of the lane.

If the alternate hand exchange method is introduced to the young athletes it can become very confusing, as problems arise when the running order is changed and they may be unaware in which hand to receive the baton and on which side of the lane to stand. For young athletes a 50–100 metres relay leg is quite a long distance to run if the baton is not in their preferred hand. Therefore, the method of swapping the baton from right hand to left or vice-versa whilst running is not necessarily a bad practice.

Young athletes also like clear and precise instructions, so what is easier than saying 'give with the left and take with the right hand' and 'swap hands whilst running'? It also overcomes the problem of the hand creeping up the baton and everyone does the same no matter which leg is run which is very useful in linear relays. These are additional reasons for supporting the change of baton hand whilst running. The safe exchange is far more important than gaining a few hundredths of a second, if anything is gained at all. However, it must be reiterated that when the athletes are older, advantages can be gained from improved take-over methods.

The take-over of the baton should be a 'blind exchange' by the outgoing runner which implies that he or she must not look back for the baton. Correct timing is imperative and it is essential that the outgoing runner does not outrun the incoming runner. As familiarity and timing improve, the take-over technique can be refined.

6.7 Relay Practices Using the Upsweep Pass

6.7.1 The 'Outgoing' Runner
The 'outgoing' runner holds the hand in which the baton will be received downwards with the arm sloping slightly backwards. An inverted 'V' made between the thumb and the fingers will be presented into which the 'incoming' runner will place the baton with an upwards motion. It is most important that the 'V' is in line with the baton and clearly visible to the 'incoming' runner. The 'outgoing' runner must focus forward at all times when receiving the baton.

6.7.2 The 'Incoming' Runner

It is the responsibility of the 'incoming' runner to ensure exchange of the baton takes place as only he or she can see what is actually happening. The 'incoming' runner passes the baton firmly into the 'V' of the 'outgoing' runner's hand. The hands of both runners should touch, so that as much of the baton as possible is available for the next take-over.

6.7.3 Changing the Baton Hand whilst Running
If the method of changing the baton hand whilst running is to be taught, the outgoing runner should change the baton as soon as possible after receiving it. If it is carried out at this point, the young athlete can get into full sprinting action without still having to think about changing the baton hand. There is a hidden value in using this method with young athletes as observation shows that relaxation occurs when changing the baton from one hand to the other hand which is not always an easy skill for sprinters.

6.7.4 The Check Mark

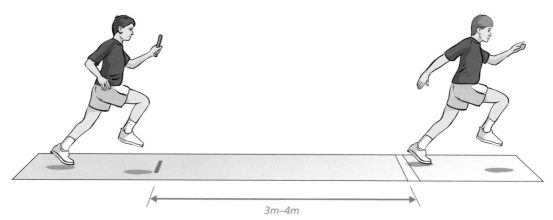

3m–4m

The outgoing runner should measure out and place a check mark to denote when to begin running as the incoming runner hits the check mark. There is not a set distance for the check mark and it will be determined by the speed of the incoming runner against the speed of the outgoing runner. If the incoming runner cannot catch the outgoing runner the check mark is too far away and if the incoming runner sprints past the outgoing runner the check mark is too close.

Perfecting the check mark distance will take a lot of practice over the full distance of the relay.

6.8 Speed Games & Relays

	SCHEDULE OF RELAYS	VENUE APPROPRIATENESS					EQUIPMENT (assumed cones available)						
		INDOOR	PLAYGROUND	FIELD OR CENTRE OF TRACK	ALL WEATHER	TRACK	BATONS	TWO-WAY PLASTIC FOLDING HURDLES	BEAN BAGS	TUNNELS	GYM MATS	HOOPS	TASK AND OBSTACLE ITEMS
LINEAR RELAYS	Gathering Relay	✔	✔	✔	✔	✔			✔			✔	
	Task Relay	✔	✗	✔	✗	✗							✔
	Skipping Relay	✔	✔	✔	✗	✔							✔
	Memory Relay	✔	✔	✔	✔	✔			✔				✔
SMALL CIRCULAR RELAYS	Partner Pursuit	✔	✔	✔	✔	✔							
	'All In' Relay	✔	✔	✔	✔	✔	✔						
	Pursuit Relay	✔	✔	✔	✔	✔	✔						
	Tag Relay	✔	✔	✔	✔	✔	✔						
	Knockout Tag Relay	✔	✔	✔	✔	✔	✔						
	Over Under Tag Relay	✔	✗	✔	✗	✗		✔		✔	✔		

The Linear Relays can be performed either indoors or outdoors. If they take place indoors 'reversaboards' should be used and for outdoors the 'reversaboards' can be replaced with cones. It is a very important safety factor that only two-way plastic folding hurdles are used for these relays and not standard track hurdles.

6.8.1 Linear Relays

6.8.1.1 Gathering Relay

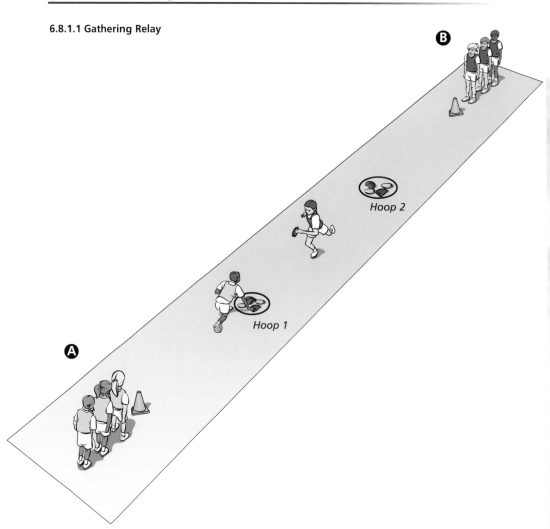

Activity: The first member of Team 'A' runs to collect a beanbag from Hoop '1' and drops it into Hoop '2'. At the same time, the first member of Team 'B' collects a beanbag from Hoop '2' and drops it into Hoop '1'. This continues over a specified time period and the winning team is the one with the most beanbags in the dropping hoop.

6.8.1.2 Task Relay

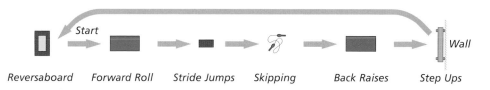

Reversaboard   Forward Roll   Stride Jumps   Skipping   Back Raises   Step Ups

Activity: Each young athlete completes one lap of the course, attempting the task on the way out and sprinting on the return. The first team member starts on the whistle with a forward roll, which should be performed from a kneeling position with both hands on the mat. He or she then completes a series of tasks such as:

- Stride Jumps on to a box
- Skipping with a rope
- Back Raises
- Step-ups on to a bench

On the return run the athlete does not attempt any of the tasks but must sprint back and turn on the reversaboard before touching the shoulder of the next athlete who is crouched in front of the team mat for takeover. All team members complete this sequence but, after turning on the reversaboard the last runner must sprint to the finish line, which can be situated where the skipping rope was initially placed.

Use monitors or parents for the following safety duties:

(a) Sitting on stride box and counting the strides. This ensures that the box does not move.
(b) Counting the skips and gathering the rope.
(c) Holding the feet for back raises and counting.
(d) Sitting on the step-up bench and counting. This ensures the bench does not move.

The same monitor can do all four jobs by moving along with the athlete.

6.8.1.3 Skipping Relay

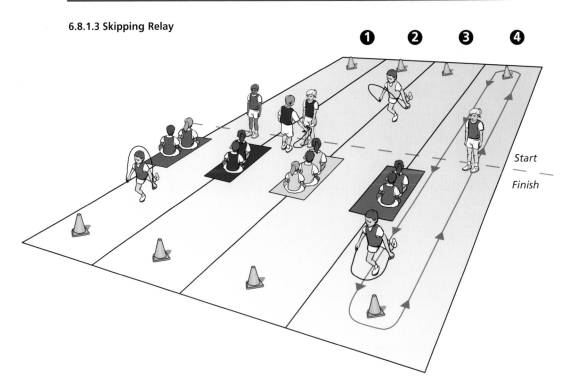

Activity: The start and finish of this type of relay is the halfway point between the two cones. Waiting team members sit on their team mat to the side of their lane. A complete lap is the distance from the start / finish line to the first cone followed by the full length of the course to the return cone and back to the start / finish line. The first runner stands behind the start line facing the numbered cone. On the whistle, the first runner completes one lap skipping continuously. The take-over is by passing the skipping rope to the next team member. After exchanging the skipping rope the runner sits on the team mat and the last runner finishes the relay by crossing the start / finish line at the end of his or her lap.

6.8.1.4 Memory Relay

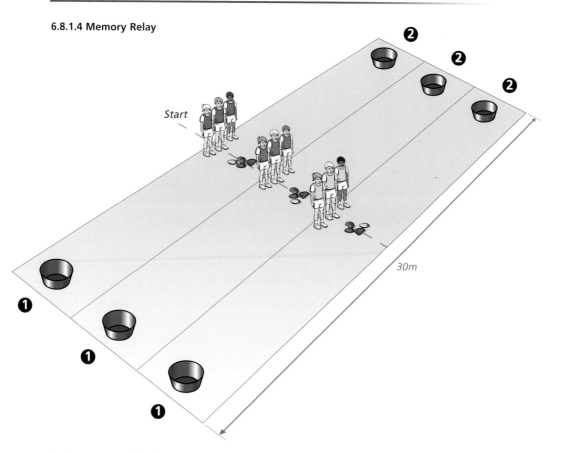

Activity: Any number from two to four can be in a team. Each team is positioned at the centre of the course in a lane or distinct clear running area. At either end of each team's lane is placed a bucket or tub. The relay is under the control of a caller who calls instructions in a loud, clear voice. The tubs are designated '1' and '2' and four coloured bean bags are allocated to each team and placed at the centre. The starting sequence is as follows:
'Red to 2'
and the team members must take the red bag to tub '2'.

This can be followed by 'Blue to 1' and the blue bag must be taken to tub '1'. The caller follows by instructing the teams to place the yellow and green bags in tubs so that all four bags are in tubs. There could be two in each tub or three in one and one in the other - it does not matter.

The caller shouts a colour and the team must remember which tub that it was in and send a member to get it and transfer it to the other tub. The quickest team gets a point. The pace can get quite fast and teams can get quite confused for they must remember where the colours are.

6.8.2. Small Circular Relays
6.8.2.1 Partner Pursuit

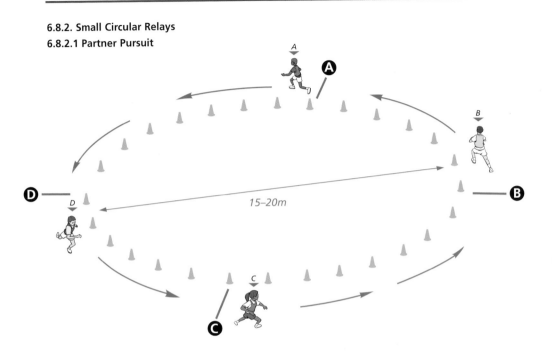

15–20m

Activity: One young athlete starts at the opposite side of the track to his or her partner and they attempt to catch each other in a pursuit around the circuit.

One pair of young athletes could start at points 'A' and 'C' and another pair at points 'B' and 'D'. They must be instructed to run either clockwise or anti-clockwise and a time limit should be set on the chase.

The circle should only be 15–20 metres diameter and a maximum number of laps of twelve should be applied. If one catches the other, the trial is over. More than one pair can run at a time, each chasing his or her own partner. There are lots of things to be touched upon like maintaining a 'steady pace', 'speeding up' and 'recovery'.

Please note that the diameters of these tracks may be reduced for indoor use and will be dependent on the size of the facility. It is a very important to ensure the track allows the young athletes to run safely without colliding with walls or pieces of equipment. Therefore the track should be marked out with these safety considerations in mind.

6.8.2.2 'All In' Relay

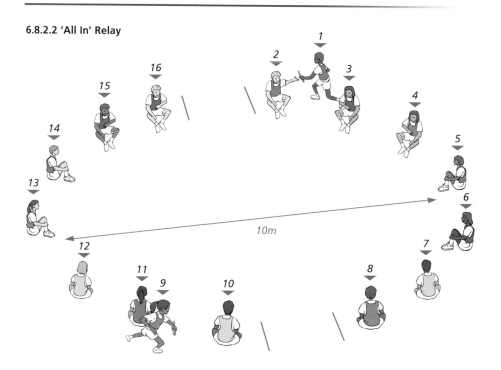

Activity: All young athletes are asked to sit down in a circle and large numbers can take part. The diagram shows a circle of sixteen young athletes.

Young athlete No. 1 is given a baton and runs around the circle before passing it to young athlete No. 2. No. 1 then sits down in the original place and 2 continues the relay before passing to No. 3.

At the same time, a baton is given to say No. 9, who runs around and passes to No. 10 so two relays are in process at the same time and all the young athletes are involved in each team.

There is no reason why three or more starting positions cannot be used. Circles can involve up to sixty young athletes on a large field with six batons being relayed.

Please note that the diameters of these tracks may be reduced for indoor use and will be dependent on the size of the facility. It is a very important to ensure the track allows the young athletes to run safely without colliding with walls or pieces of equipment. Therefore the track should be marked out with these safety considerations in mind.

6.8.2.3 Pursuit Relay

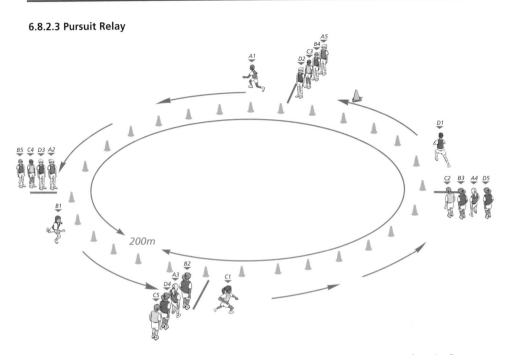

Activity: Each team is given a letter and each team member is given a number. Therefore the first member of team 'A' is 'A1' and the fifth member of team 'A' is 'A5'. All the first members of each team are given a baton and when the whistle is blown they run anti-clockwise, so that 'A1' passes the baton to 'A2' who passes the baton to 'A3' and so on.

Team 'A' is chasing Team 'B'

Team 'B' is chasing Team 'C'

Team 'C' is chasing Team 'D'

Team 'D' is chasing Team 'A'

All four teams are chasing around together and passing the baton at every take-over. When the baton reaches the fifth runners they continue passing it on again to the first, second and third and so on, round and round until the fifth runners are back in their starting places at which point the batons are held aloft to indicate that the team has finished. All members of all teams should have run four times and each team would have covered five laps.

6.8.2.4 Tag Relay

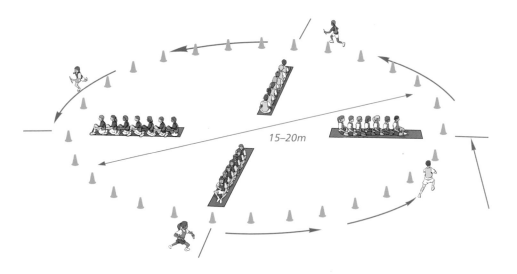

15–20m

Activity: Each runner runs one lap before passing the baton onto the next member who must be ready. The chase continues until someone catches the team in front and 'Tags' them with the baton. The whistle blows - all running stops and a point is awarded to the team making the 'Tag'. The two teams involved in the 'Tag' change places and the chase starts again.

For example, if team 'A' catches team 'B' the whistle blows, all stop and team 'A' are awarded one point. Then 'A' and 'B' change places so that 'A' is chasing 'C', 'C' is chasing 'D' and 'D' is chasing 'B'.

When appropriate, the 'referee' can change the running direction from 'anti-clockwise' to 'clockwise' or have the scoring team change mats with the team it caught. The teams do not necessarily require the same number so no young athlete is left out.

Please note that the diameters of these tracks may be reduced for indoor use and will be dependent on the size of the facility. It is a very important to ensure the track allows the young athletes to run safely without colliding with walls or pieces of equipment. Therefore the track should be marked out with these safety considerations in mind.

6.8.2.5 Knockout Tag Relay

Activity: This is run along similar lines to the Tag Relay but when a team is 'tagged' with the baton it drops out. When the first team is eliminated, leaving three teams in the chase, the starting positions are altered to ensure all teams are an equal distance apart. The chase continues and eventually a second team is eliminated making it a final duel. Again the starting positions should be altered and the course reduced in size to allow the teams a fair chance of catching one another.

It is best that the teams have at least six members and preferably seven or eight. A time limit of 2 or 3 minutes should be applied because with well-balanced teams, the chase can go on for a considerable period of time. The chase is continuous so after the last member of each team has run his or her first lap, the first member runs again and so on.

6.8.2.6 Over Under Tag Relay

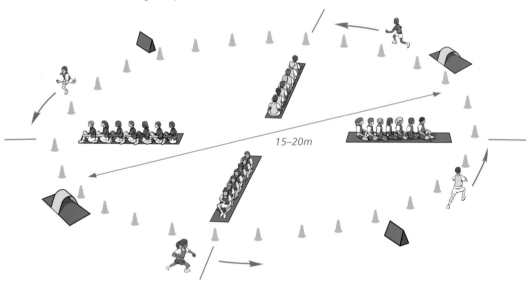

15–20m

Activity: The same rules apply as those explained for the Tag Relay but the young athletes must attempt to clear the hurdles and go through the tunnels and for safety a bean bag is used in place of a relay baton.

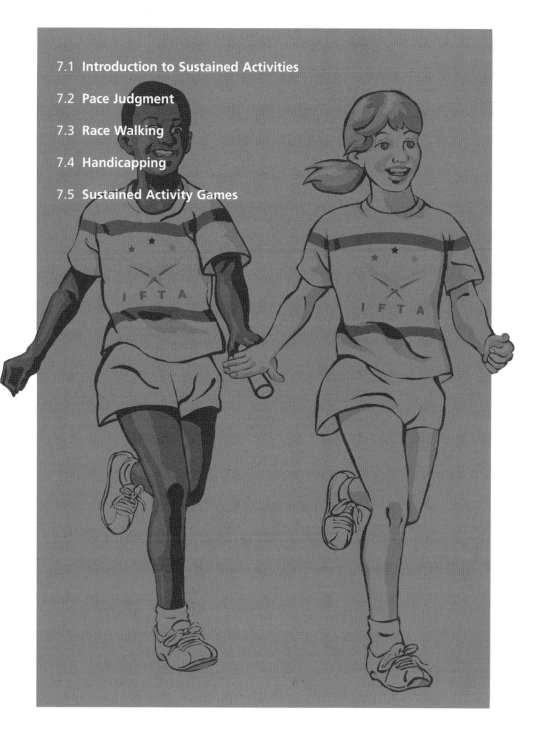

7.1 Introduction to Sustained Activities

There are two different forms of competitive sustained activities in athletics, namely running and walking, and these take place on many different kinds of terrain.

Running
Cross-Country
Hill and Fell
Road
Track

Walking
Road
Track

It is advisable, when coaching young athletes under 13 years old, that activity sessions take place on the track, on playing fields or over country. Hill and Fell and Road terrains can be very hazardous for large groups of young athletes. Additional skills are required by a coach to ensure safety in traffic and to anticipate rapid climate changes in the hills etc. Running on roads can also cause joint problems, especially in the knees, for young athletes who are in a period of growth development.

It is a well-recognised phenomenon that a young athlete will respond very quickly to training for a particular discipline but this may not be in his or her best long-term interests. In general, it is recommended that a maximum of two sessions per week, determined by the strength of the young athlete, is more than adequate. Even then the emphasis should be on speed endurance rather than encouraging over-distance runs. Young athletes' bodies adapt differently than adults bodies do during sustained activities and overheating can easily occur. Therefore, sessions should mainly consist of pace running, relaxed running and breathing pattern to the rhythm of strides.

Section 7.2 is dedicated primarily to pace judgment in relation to sustained activities that can take place on a track or can be adapted to grassland. Several practical ideas are offered as a guide to good practice.

7.1.1 Cross-Country

Cross-Country can be an enjoyable activity for all, but it should not be compulsory that young athletes participate. In addition to being an event in itself Cross-Country will provide an excellent groundwork for cardiovascular fitness and strength endurance for other events. Cross-Country should not be restricted to being a winter activity as summer events and runs can be most enjoyable and provide variations to training sessions.

A wide variety of facilities present themselves as ideal for Cross-Country from urban parkland, open country and woodland to running along the beach. Under 13 year olds should not be allowed to undertake unsupervised Cross-Country runs for reasons of safety and / or avoiding injury. Young athletes must always be accompanied by a coach or a suitably experienced senior athlete, who will be working under the direction of the coach.

Relaxed runs with varied effort are best so that young athletes can cope with the distance and not become distressed through over-exertion. Coaches should encourage use of the terrain to assist free and relaxed running without struggling. It is best if Cross-Country for under 13 year olds is held in the form of team events or relays. Coaches and parents need to be positive and supportive at all times.

The maximum distances recommended for Cross-Country events for young athletes are:

- Girls and Boys Under 13 years and Over 11 years   3000 metres
- Girls and Boys Under 11 years   2000 metres
- Girls and Boys Under 9 years   1500 metres

7.1.2 Track

Many organised track & field competitions incorporate within their programmes 600 metres to 1500 metres races for young athletes under 13 years old. There is nothing wrong with young athletes running these distances but it is important not to simulate the intensive training schedules that these events would require for older athletes.

I·F·T·A

7.2 Pace Judgment

Learning the skill of pace judgment is quite a challenge for most children, indeed, a high percentage of young athletes and sometimes even elite athletes set off far too quickly in endurance activities and many find themselves distressed after a short period of time.

It is important for the coach always to work within the capability of each young athlete and not to push him or her to achieve unrealistic times set by the fastest in the group. For example, a very good 12 year old may be recording around 2 minutes 32 seconds for 800 metres whilst other good club members may be capable of around 3 minutes. The coach needs to recognise these different ability levels and be careful to ensure that young athletes are working at their own pace.

7.2.1 Practical Application of Pace Judgment

The purpose of the following exercise is not to set new targets but to teach young athletes economy and self-control over the distance they are running. The application of control will improve performance with a more even expenditure of effort.

7.2.1.1 Pace Run - Introduction

'Pace Schedules' for 800 metres and 1500 metres showing split times for even pace running are shown in Section 7.2.1.5.

The aim is to help achieve times in competition so in training young athletes using the 800m pace schedule should not exceed 400m runs and 1500m trials should be run over a maximum of 600m. These maximum distances should only be attempted after a gradual build-up to achieve cardio-vascular fitness and confidence in the young athletes ability. For athletes under 11 years it may be advisable to further sub-divide the 'Pace Schedules' into 50 metres segments rather than just the 100 metres segments.

Emphasise to young athletes that they are not to race and must try to keep within their own individually allocated pace schedule. Provided the target times have been set correctly the young athletes will be running within their own capabilities and they will recover very quickly. However, a sufficient rest period should always be given between trials.

When a young athlete has become experienced in pace judgment through training sessions, he or she can then be allowed to participate in a time-trial on an individual basis, this is done over at least two-thirds and not more than three-quarters of the competition distance. Therefore young athletes wishing to compete at the 800m will participate in a 600m time-trial and those wishing to compete at the 1500m will participate in a 1000m time-trial. Again, the 'Pace Schedules' for these distances can be seen in Section 7.2.1.5. If the young athletes can run comfortably and hit their given 'Pace Schedule' in these time-trials, they should be confident of achieving their target times during competitions.

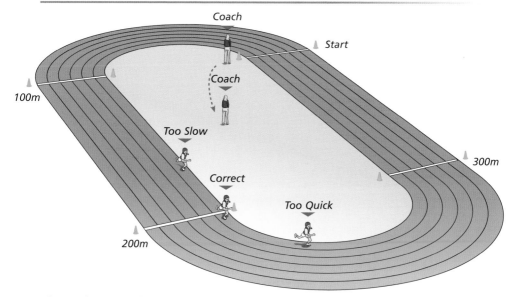

The coach may need to move into a position where he or she can get a better view of the young athletes.

7.2.1.2 Pace Run - Stage One

- Place a cone at the 100 metres mark on the track
- Group the athletes in pairs of similar ability and select an appropriate 'pace schedule' for each pair. For example, one young athlete may have a personal best of 2 minutes 49 seconds for the 800 metres and the other may have a personal best of 2 minutes 53 seconds. It is advisable for these young athletes to work to a 'pace schedule' of 2 minutes 48 seconds as this is nearest an even pace schedule split below their personal best. If they are running at the right pace to achieve 2 minutes 48 seconds they must reach the 100 metres cone in 21 seconds.
- Remind the athletes that it is **not a race** but an exercise in pace judgment and they should note where they are in relation to the first cone when the whistle is blown to check their position.
- Using a run through start 10 metres back from the start line, start the stopwatch as the runners pass the start line.
- Blow the whistle after 21 seconds and note the point reached.
- Each pair within the group takes its turn at its own 'pace schedule'.
- When it is the turn of the first pair to run again, ensure that the young athletes have had an adequate rest period. Before each group starts its next run, advise its members whether they should increase or decrease their speed from the previous effort. This may take a complete session to master but it is very important that they become consistent in the very early stages of pace judgment training.

7.2.1.3 Pace Run - Stage Two
- Place cones at the 100 and 200 metres marks on the track.
- Using the example described in Stage One, extend the distance to 200 metres with the aim of reaching the 200 metre cone in 42 seconds.
- Blow the whistle at the halfway point of 21 seconds. The young athlete should continue to run but check how close he or she is to the 100 metre cone.
- Blow the whistle after 42 seconds when the runners should be very close to the 200 metres cone if their pace judgment is accurate.

7.2.1.4 Pace Run - Stage Three & Four
Stage Three progresses to a 300 metres run with two intermediate checks at 100 and 200 metres and all stages marked for visibility by a cone. Stage Four is the final stage for 800 metres training, which is a 400 metres pace run with intermediate checks every 100 metres.

Young athletes who master pace judgment are much more confident in their ability and can, by applying good tactics, defeat stronger athletes. They also enjoy the non-stressful training sessions, which is psychologically better for them than highly intense activity. When young athletes become familiar with the principle of pace judgment training they can help the coach by working in a group and doing their own timing, whistle blowing and checking the distances run.

Young athletes should be running well within their capabilities and the following session is suggested for a one hour activity session for 800 metres training. It should be performed at the 'pace schedule' speeds shown in 7.2.1.5

7.2.1.5 Training Sessions
Athletes must be fresh if they are to benefit when involved in pace judgement training. The exercise is of no value to a tired runner.

The first introductory session will probably involve five or six trials over distances of 100 and 200 metres with rest breaks of five to ten minutes between each trial. The runners will be running well within their capacity so they will recover quickly. In this introductory session the use of intermediary markers positioned at 50 metres and 150 metres may be beneficial.

The athlete will quickly develop a fair idea of the required pace so in future sessions the trial distances should be extended to 300 metres and 400 metres with rest periods between each trial of about 15 minutes. When carrying out trials over distances beyond 100 metres should the runner not be within close proximity to check point when the whistle is blown then it is pointless them continuing and the coach should signal them to stop by blowing a long blast on the whistle

Pace judgement is precision work.

7.2.1.6 Pace Schedules

800 metres EVEN PACE RUNNING TIMES									
	m s	m s	m s	m s	m s	m s	m s	m s	m s
800m	2.24	2.32	2.40	2.48	2.56	3.04	3.12	3.20	3.28
Splits For Even Pace									
100m	.18	.19	.20	.21	.22	.23	.24	.25	.26
200m	.36	.38	.40	.42	.44	.46	.48	.50	.52
300m	.54	.57	1.00	1.03	1.06	1.09	1.12	1.15	1.18
400m	1.12	1.16	1.20	1.24	1.28	1.32	1.38	1.40	1.44
*600m		1.48	1.54	2.00	2.06	2.12	2.18	2.24	2.30 2.36

1500 metres EVEN PACE RUNNING TIMES									
	m s	m s	m s	m s	m s	m s	m s	m s	m s
1500m	4.45	5.00	5.15	5.30	5.45	6.00	6.15	6.30	6.45
Splits For Even Pace									
100m	.19	.20	.21	.22	.23	.24	.25	.26	.27
200m	.38	.40	.42	.44	.46	.48	.50	.52	.54
300m	.57	1.00	1.03	1.06	1.09	1.12	1.15	1.18	1.21
400m	1.16	1.20	1.24	1.28	1.32	1.36	1.40	1.44	1.48
500m	1.35	1.40	1.45	1.50	1.55	2.00	2.05	2.10	2.15
600m	1.54	2.00	2.06	2.12	2.18	2.24	2.30	2.36	2.42
*1000m	3.10	3.20	3.30	3.40	3.50	4.00	4.10	4.20	4.30

* these distances should be run on an individual time-trial basis

Please note it is advisable for the young athlete to work at the pace schedule of the nearest time below his or her personal best.

7.3 Race Walking

Walking can be lots of fun and is particularly suitable if introduced to young athletes as a game as it enables large numbers to take part in a simple sustained activity. It is recommended that only the basic concept of walking is introduced to the under 13 age group and therefore the initial emphasis should be on walking in a straight line and maintaining unbroken contact with the ground.

The basic requirement is that one foot must be in contact with the ground at all times.
The technique adopted is one in which the walker strikes the ground on each step with the heel of the forward foot and the leg straight, pushing on that foot through to the toe to increase stride length and driving forward.

7.3.1 The Feet
Emphasis must be on placing the inside of the heel on the ground and walking with the inside edge of the shoe along the line of progression. For this practice the lane marking lines on a track are very useful. The whole foot must be brought into action and the walker must feel that he or she is pushing off the ball and toes of one foot onto the heel of the other.

7.3.2 The Knees
The knee needs to be straightened vigorously as the leg passes under the hips to push off onto the other foot. The general impression here is of an extension at the hip, knee and ankle with a push off the ball and toes of the foot.

7.3.3 The Trunk

The back and abdominal muscles must be strong as there is considerable involvement of these groups in maintaining a solid, erect posture. The back must be straight but remain relaxed to ensure tension is not created in the body and to ensure maximum efficiency in the technique.

7.3.4 The Hips

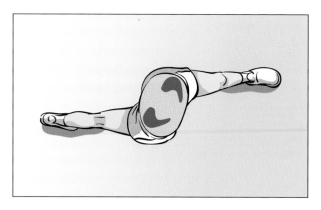

The hips should be swung well forward to enhance the stride length but at the same time the hips should simulate a wave-like motion reaching a high point when the supporting leg is straightened in the vertical position and a low point during the recovery when it passes the straightened leg. This helps to avoid total rise and fall of the body, therefore keeping the centre of gravity fairly constant.

7.3.5 The Shoulders and Arms

A powerful arm action should be used to drive the body and legs forward. The action is over a wide range and the elbows should be maintained as near as possible to the body at 90° flexion. The elbow should be pulled high behind the body and the arms should swing across in front of the body. Shoulders should be kept square to the direction of the movement.

7.3.6 The Head

The eyes should be fixed forward (about 10m–20m ahead), head steady and neck muscles relaxed. The head must not be allowed to roll from side to side at any point as this may lead to inefficiency in the rest of the technique.

7.3.7 Group Observation

Having carefully explained the basic technique of race walking, the young athletes can work with partners or small groups and observe each other's actions.

- Is your partner maintaining contact with the ground?
- Is your partner holding the trunk and head erect or is he or she leaning forwards or backwards?
- Is the head rolling from side-to-side?
- Is your partner keeping the knee straight after planting the heel?
- Is your partner using the hips correctly?
- Could your partner increase his or her stride length?
- Are your partner's shoulders being kept square?
- Does your partner have good arm swing?

Young athletes who have developed a good walking technique can be asked to demonstrate their technique to their peers.

7.3.8 Summary of Technique

i) One foot must be in contact with the ground at all times.

ii) Head and trunk to be kept upright.

iii) Strike the ground with the heel of the foot and ensure a straight leg action.

iv) Push from foot up to the toes, to increase stride length.

v) Hip action - maintain the swinging forward.

vi) Arm action - prevent over-swing.

7.4 Handicapping

The purpose of a handicap event is to give all the competitors an even chance of winning whatever their ability. In a perfect handicap race all the runners would reach the finishing line at the same time. However, in practice it is seldom the case, although we do get close finishes.

There are basically two methods of handicapping athletes for track and cross-country races:

a) Handicapping by staggering the distances from which a competitor starts.

b) Handicapping by staggering the time at which the competitor starts.

Method (a) is normally applied to sprint handicaps and middle distance races up to 1000 metres while method (b) is simpler and more practical for distances from 1200 metres upwards on the track and it is also used for road and cross-country.

7.4.1 Handicapping by Distance

The IFTA 800 metres handicapping tables can be seen in section 7.4.2 and are provided as a guide to assist coaches to establish a handicap programme. They give the recommended starting position measuring forward from the scratch line and fixed according to the ability of the runner.

The tables provide for young athletes in a range of ability bands. The recommended staggers have been adjusted into simple steps of 10 metres apart from in level 4, which would only apply to young athletes capable of very high performances. Using this method it must be realised that the stagger from the scratch line should be related to the pace of the athlete to whom the handicap is being applied.

For example, consider the level 2 handicap for a young athlete capable of running 800 metres in 2 minutes 40 seconds. This runner would move at a pace of 5 metres per second and as he or she would take 16 seconds longer to cover the distance than a 2 minutes 24 seconds scratch runner the starting position is set forward from the scratch line by 80 metres (16 seconds x 5 metres per second).

This criteria have been used to create the scales for levels 1, 2 and 3 and the "in-between" staggers have been evened out for simplification. However, as can be seen for level 4 a stricter criterion has been applied.

7.4.2 IFTA Handicaps for 800 Metres

Metres per sec	Level 4 Handicaps		Level 3 Handicaps		Level 2 Handicaps		Level 1 Handicaps	
Pace	Time	Metres*	Time	Metres*	Time	Metres*	Time	Metres*
6.67	2.00	Scratch						
	2.01	7						
	2.02	13						
	2.03	20						
	2.04	26						
6.40	2.05	32						
	2.06	38						
	2.07	45						
	2.09	55						
	2.10.5	65						
6.04	2.12.5	75	2.12	Scratch				
	2.14	85	2.14	10				
	2.16	95	2.16	20				
	2.18	105	2.18	30				
5.71	2.20	115	2.20	40				
	2.22	125	2.22	50				
		Limit	2.24	60	2.24	Scratch		
			2.26	70	2.26	10		
			2.28	80	2.28	20		
5.33			2.30	90	2.30	30		
			2.32	100	2.32	40		
			2.34	110	2.34	50		
			2.36	120	2.36	60		
			2.38	125	2.38	70		
5.00				Limit	2.40	80	2.40	Scratch
					2.42	90	2.42	10
					2.44	100	2.44	20
					2.46	110	2.46	30
					2.48	120	2.48	40
4.71					2.50	125	2.50	50
						Limit	2.53	60
							2.56	70
							2.59	80
4.40							3.02	90
							3.04	100
							3.06	110
							3.08	120
							3.10	125
4.21								Limit
Handicaps allowances are measured forward from the scratch line								

*Allowance in metres

7.4.3 Allocating Handicaps

The tables in 7.4.2 should be used as a guideline for fixing handicaps at the start of a season's programme or when a new member joins. Should a regular programme of handicapped races be established then the following tips may be useful:

- Award points for each race to the first six places.
- Apply penalties to the first three in the race according to their finishing positions (For example, 15 metres, 10 metres and 5 metres).
- The coach can use discretion as to whether anyone is moved forward for the next race but be alert to anyone working his or her handicap.
- Have a special set of pre-marked cones to set alongside the starting positions of each young athlete.

7.4.4 Handicapping by Staggered Starting Times

The expected performance of the weakest competitor is used as a datum to determine the scratch position and the competitors are lined up in file behind this member in order of their ability. The timekeeper starts the watch as the first runner starts and all the following runners are set off in turn at the time estimated for them to catch the leader. The same watch can be used to record finishing times and actual times are calculated by subtracting the handicap start time.

For example, consider a number of young athletes taking part in a race over a distance of 1500 metres.

Name	Estimated Performance	Handicap in seconds
Jane	5 min 15 sec	0 secs
Mary	5 min 7 sec	8 secs
Anne	5 min 1 sec	14 secs
Julie	4 min 55 sec	20 secs
Kathy	4 min 48 sec	27 secs
Beth	4 min 42 sec	33 secs
Diane	4 min 35 sec	40 secs

As the programme progresses through the season the coach will develop a sound idea as to the correct handicap for each young athlete and may be pleasantly surprised by the improvement made by the less talented group members. Again a points system can be incorporated and the handicaps adjusted by the coach as the season progresses.

7.5 Sustained Activity Games

7.5.1 Continuous Relay (400 metres track)

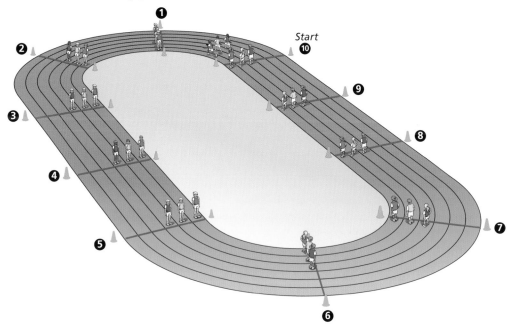

This relay is suitable for teams with six to thirteen members. If each team has eleven members then the track is divided into ten segments each measuring 40 metres. The distances between the cones is short so each team member can run several times. However, the number of laps should be variable depending upon the number of members in a team.

The diagram above illustrates three teams of eleven athletes. The first runner from each team starts the relay in his or her allocated lane and passes the baton to the runner at take-over number one who runs in his or her allocated lane and passes to the runner at take-over number two. At this point the young athletes can 'break' and run in lane one. The baton continues to be passed to the next runner in each team until the baton reaches the runner at take-over number ten who starts the next lap and passes to the first runner. The relay continues until the declared number of laps has been completed.

As an alternative, realistic time targets can be set based on known and achievable records. These might be a world record, a National record or an age group record over 1500 or 3000 metres.

7.5.2 3000 metres Continuous Relay (seven and half laps of a 400 metres track)

This continuous relay has been devised for teams of ten members consisting of five girls and five boys of whom one member should be appointed as team captain. The combined age of the team must not exceed a total of 100 years for nine team members excluding the captain who must be under 16 years of age.

The relay commences with the captains completing a 200 metres section run in lanes. They then pass the baton onto the next runners positioned at 'take-over A' which will be the break point from where all teams no longer have to run in lanes. From here, the other nine members of the team will continue to run in sequence over 50 metres sections, passing the baton onto their next team member at the take-over points. Each of these nine members will run six times and therefore complete a total distance of 300 metres and the baton will then be at take-over point G, from where the captains will be required to run the final 100 metres to the finish.

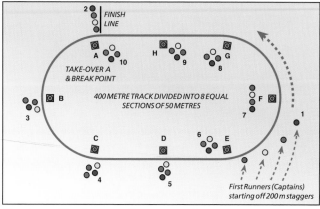

Team:			
Team No.	Name	Boy or Girl	Age
Captain			
2			
3			
4			
5			
6			
7			
8			
9			
10			
Total age for team members 2–9 must not exceed 100 years			

7.5.3 Walking – One Minute Team Challenge

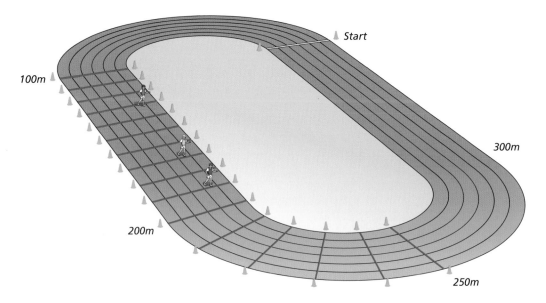

Using a 400 metres track place a cone at the start line and add an additional cone every 10 metres from 100 metres point to the 250 metres point on the lap. Young athletes should work in groups and each group member will be challenged to see how far they can walk in 1 minute.

The recorder starts the young athlete with a whistle and they set off walking around the track to see which cone they can reach before a second whistle is blown after one minute. Young athletes can be placed as observers around the track to judge that the walker is maintaining contact with the ground and not 'lifting', the term used when continuous contact with the ground is broken. When the whistle blows the second time the recorder notes which cone the walker had reached and writes it on the record sheet, which has increments of 10 metres.

The group can be split into teams of four, five, six or seven members and a team competition can be held as follows:

The first member of each team is tested to see how far he or she can walk in 1 minute and the achievement recorded, provided there is no disqualification for 'lifting'. The second members of each team then compete to see how far they can achieve. The coach can decide to score the aggregate of the best three, four, five or six from each team. If the best four from each team of six or seven were to score the competition results could look like the those on the following sample scorecard:

RED TEAM			BLUE TEAM			YELLOW TEAM		
Name	Dist.	Best 4	Name	Dist	Best 4	Name	Dist.	Best 4
1 Billy	160	-	1 Anne	170	-	1 Sophie	180	180
2 John	190	190	2 Les	160	-	2 Maria	200	200
3 Jane	190	190	3 George	180	180	3 Will	160	-
4 Alison	210	210	4 John	210	210	4 Bob	200	200
5 Frank	160	-	5 Ian	200	200	5 Alan	150	-
6 Bobby	170	-	6 Violet	180	180	6 June	160	-
7 Paul	190	190	7 -	-	-	7 Janet	170	170
Score		780	Score		770	Score		750

7.5.4 Walking for Distance – Linear Track

This activity can be carried out either on a linear track or on a mini track (see 7.4.4) and the aim of the activity is to walk as far as possible in a set time period. Using a linear track or mini track compared to using a full 400 metres track can be very beneficial to both the coach and the young athlete in this type of activity. The coach is always close to the young athletes and can therefore observe any distress they may be experiencing and act accordingly. It can also be a psychological advantage to the young athletes that they are always close to other young athletes regardless of walking or running ability.

The layout for the linear track is as follows:

A series of cones is placed 10 metres apart with the exception of the two end cones, which are placed at 9 metres to compensate for the young athlete turning when taking part in the activity.

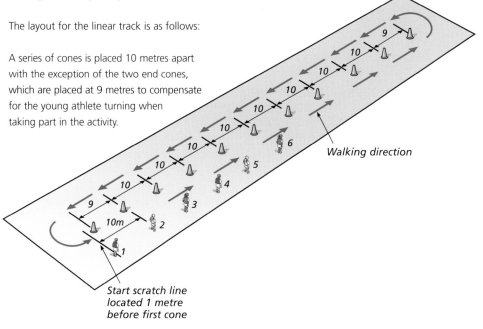

Walking direction

Start scratch line located 1 metre before first cone

148

I·F·T·A

The young athletes start and finish on a whistle for a specified time period (up to a maximum of 10 minutes). The illustration above shows the recommended starting positions for six young athletes participating in the activity. A recording sheet has been designed to assist the coach in measuring the distance achieved by individual young athletes.

Name	Starting Adjustment (metres)	200m	200m	200m	200m	200m	200m	200m	200m	Finishing Adjustment (metres)	Distance Achieved (metres)	Penalties (metres)	Total Distance (metres)
Steve Jones	-10	✔	✔	✔	✔	30				20	820	80	740

Walking Distance Against a Fixed Time Period (5 minutes)

100 metres Linear Track = 200 metres per lap

In the table above the Total Distance for the young athlete was calculated as follows:

Steve Jones started at position no. 2 on the illustration of the Layout of the Linear Track. He then completed Four full laps of the track (from the Scratch Line) and an extra 30 metres before the whistle was blown for the 5 minute time period. His finishing adjustment was 20 metres because of the fact that he started 10 metres in front of the Scratch Line. He obtained 80 metres of Penalties and therefore his Total Distance was calculated by subtracting the Penalties from the Distance Achieved.

It is important with all the games activities that the young athlete is encouraged to learn the skill correctly and therefore it is suggested that penalties rather than disqualification for an illegal walking technique are applied . Therefore, the coach or other young athletes acting as judges can be given yellow and red cards that can be shown to the participating young athletes for a caution or a foul.

The penalties for illegal 'lifting' techniques should be applied as follows:

Fault	Young Athlete Shown	Penalty
Caution	Yellow Card	20 metres
Foul	Red Card	40 metres

7.5.5 Running for Distance – Mini Tack

The layout for the mini track is as follows:

A series of ten cones is placed as shown below with the 5 metres radius on the bend being measured to the centre of the cones. Such a track will give an effective measurement of approximately 50 metres, as the young athletes will be running or walking around the outside of the cones, which create ten segments of 5 metres.

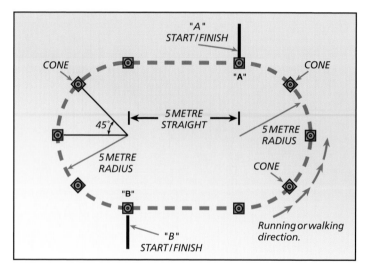

One young athlete will start at position A and the other young athlete at position B. They start and finish on a whistle and compete for a specified time period (up to a maximum of 10 minutes). Once again their individual total distance can be recorded by the number of laps completed (50 metres per lap) plus the number of 5 metres segments completed for the final incomplete lap when the whistle is blown.

7.5.6 30, 40, 50 Club

The 30, 40, 50 Club is an initiative that has been devised and implemented very successfully by the Athletics Association of Wales. Basically it allows the young athletes to achieve distance running or walking awards without undue pressure put on them.

To carry out this activity, a one-mile course should be measured and marked out on, for example, a field, school playground or park. Each young athlete is given a record card and encouraged to gain stamps on the card for each one-mile that is completed. However, to ensure that the young athlete is not over-trained, he or she is only allowed to complete the one-mile course a maximum of twice in any one week period. Therefore, to become a member of the 30 Club it will take the young athlete a minimum of 15 weeks to attain this status, 20 weeks to become a member of the 40 Club and 25 weeks to become a member of the 50 Club. This is an excellent idea to encourage and motivate young athletes with sustained activities and will assist in ensuring a modest level of physical fitness.

8.1 Orienteering Games

8.1 Orienteering Games

8.1 Orienteering Games

Orienteering is an excellent alternative activity, especially when the weather is cold and / or wet. The activity can take place on a field, playground or within the confines of a track providing that no other activities are taking place. Although the following activities are not strictly sustained activity games, the reason for their inclusion within this section is that they are classified as orienteering related games.

For the purpose of introducing young athletes to orienteering the following methods are advisable as they are very simple but fun activities:
a) Sprint Orienteering
b) Pace Orienteering
c) Pelmanism

8.1 Sprint

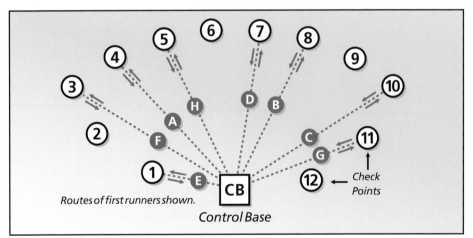

Routes of first runners shown.

Control Base

The checkpoint cards on the following pages have been designed to enable eight teams, with up to twelve members each, to take part. However, extra teams can be incorporated, if required, but for it to be a true sustained activity, team numbers should be limited to four members. If teams have four members, then each member runs three times, with six team members then each member runs twice and with twelve team members each member runs just once. All teams run the same total distance but the distance run by individual team members will vary so there is an element of chance.

Rules:
i)   Allocate each team a letter 'A' to 'H'.
ii) Each team is given a relay baton.
iii) The first members of each team should be given the reference of their first checkpoint and mark it down on the Team Card.
iv) All the first runners start together, each running to their teams' first reference checkpoint.
v)   When the first members reach the first checkpoint they must observe and remember the next checkpoint reference that is shown against the letter quoted to their team.

Example:

The first member of team 'D' is sent by the team controller to checkpoint seven and on arriving, notes the reference given against the letter 'D', which is: **D - 5**

The young athlete notes that the reference is '5' and returns to the team controller to tell both him or her and the next team member this reference. If the reference number that is brought back is wrong, the runner must return to the checkpoint to re-check the team reference number. If the reference number is correct, the team controller records it on the Team Card and the baton is exchanged. The next member then sets off to his or her allocated checkpoint.

The last member of the team will observe the letter 'F', which indicates the finish of the orienteering race, plus a 'code word' to remember and convey to the team controller. If the team has performed the orienteering activity correctly, all 12 checkpoints should have been visited in the correct sequence as given on the the Organisers' Master Check Card.

Checkpoint Cards

Checkpoint 1	Checkpoint 2	Checkpoint 3	Checkpoint 4	Checkpoint 5	Checkpoint 6
A - 12	A - 10	A - 7	A - 11	A - F	A - 1
B - 4	B - 7	B - 1	B - F	B - 11	B - 10
C - 4	C - 5	C - 12	C - 9	C - 8	C - 3
D - 6	D - 12	D - 8	D - 11	D - 2	D - 10
E - 9	E - 8	E - 12	E - 7	E - F	E - 11
F - 10	F - 11	F - 9	F - 8	F - 7	F - 1
G - 5	G - 9	G - 10	G - F	G - 12	G - 7
H - 11	H - 10	H - F	H - 12	H - 19	H - 4

Checkpoint 7	Checkpoint 8	Checkpoint 9	Checkpoint 10	Checkpoint 11	Checkpoint 12
A - 9	A - 5	A - 6	A - 8	A - 3	A - 2
B - 9	B - 5	B - 6	B - 12	B - 2	B - 3
C - 11	C - F	C - 7	C - 6	C - 2	C - 1
D - 5	D - 1	D - 4	D - F	D - 3	D - 9
E - 10	E - 5	E - 3	E - 2	E - 4	E - 6
F - 2	F - 12	F - 5	F - 4	F - 6	F - F
G - 3	G - 6	G - 1	G - 4	G - 2	G - 8
H - 1	H - 3	H - 2	H - 7	H - 6	H - 8

Team Card

TEAM NAME			TEAM LETTER	
SEQUENCE	Checkpoint 1	Start	Checkpoint 7	
	Checkpoint 2		Checkpoint 8	
	Checkpoint 3		Checkpoint 9	
	Checkpoint 4		Checkpoint 10	
	Checkpoint 5		Checkpoint 11	
	Checkpoint 6		Checkpoint 12	Finish
Time			ALL CORRECT	Yes / No

Organisers' Master Sequence Check Card

Team	Checkpoint Sequence											
	1	2	3	4	5	6	7	8	9	10	11	12
A	4	11	3	7	9	6	1	12	2	10	8	5
B	8	5	11	2	7	9	6	10	12	3	1	4
C	10	6	3	12	1	4	9	7	11	2	5	8
D	7	5	2	12	9	4	11	3	8	1	6	10
E	1	9	3	12	6	11	4	7	10	2	8	5
F	3	9	5	7	2	11	6	1	10	4	8	12
G	11	2	9	1	5	12	8	6	7	3	10	4
H	5	9	2	10	7	1	11	6	4	12	8	3

8.2 Pace Orienteering

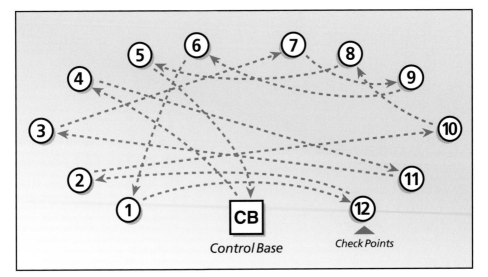

Control Base   Check Points

Within the confines of a track each team may still run over 1000m. Up to eight individuals or pairs can take part in each race A–H. You can decide on having eight individual competitors or with under 13's you can let them run with a friend so that they can help each other to judge the pace.

Assuming that you have decided pairs:

- Allocate each pair a letter (or make a draw).
- Give them a competitors card and pencil.
- Tell each pair their starting reference i.e. the first check point they visit and **mark it in square one on the competitors card**.
- Line up all eight pairs as teams at the control point and on 'go' they run to the first reference. Pair 'A' will run to checkpoint '4' where the card tells them to proceed to checkpoint '11' which they record in square '2'. At checkpoint '11' they are directed to checkpoint '3' and so on until at checkpoint '5' they are sent back to the finish.

All pairs finish at the Control Centre where their recorded sequence is checked and their time recorded.

NOTE: This is a fun event as the distance covered by each team is not quite the same. However, it is enjoyable and good training.

8.3 Pelmanism

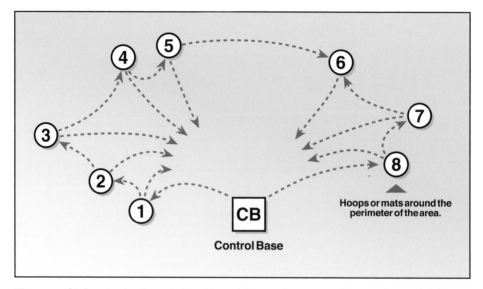

Control Base

Hoops or mats around the perimeter of the area.

The game of Pelmanism has been designed to enable up to four teams with a maximum of eight members to participate. Each team is allocated a coloured set (Red, Yellow, Green or Blue) of sixteen paired shapes. The controller retains one of each shape (using the set containing holes) from each of the teams.

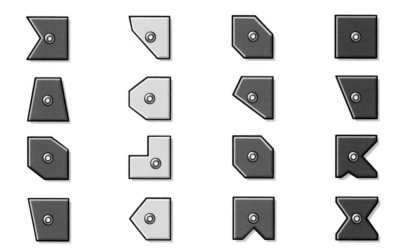

Eight hoops should be set around the perimeter of the area and the other sixteen matching shapes from each team are placed with two in each hoop. Therefore, if four teams are taking part there will be two different shapes of the four colours in each hoop.

The first competitors of each team are handed a controller's shape in the team colour and they set off to find the matching shape. If the wrong shape is brought back the competitor is sent back to replace it where it was found and to find the correct shape to make the pair.

As each young athlete successfully completes the pairing the next team member is sent out with a different controller's shape. The team has finished when all sixteen shapes have been returned to the controller in pairs. The teams should be encouraged to remember where they have already collected shapes from to save time. Tipping-off your team is permitted but each member must stay at the base unless it is his or her turn to search.

Fun in Athletics (FIA) & Sportshall Athletics (SHA)

9.1 Introduction (FIA & SHA)

9.2 Hall Layouts (FIA & SHA)

9.3 Recommended Track Events (FIA & SHA)

9.4 Recommended Field Events (FIA & SHA)

9.1 Introduction(FIA & SHA)

The original idea of Sportshall Athletics was to establish a form of winter indoor athletics competition, which could be accommodated within the confines of a sportshall or gymnasium. The concept has now been extended to include a whole range of 'Fun Athletic' activities which can also be organised outdoors. The full range of activities play an important role in many Athletic Development schemes.

Sportshall Athletics provides the opportunity for young people to take part in a form of indoor track and field activities during the winter months away from the vagaries of the weather. Participation in the activities brings the excitement and fundamental skills of track and field athletics into the school gymnasiums and leisure centres. It gives young people an introduction to athletics using specialist equipment such as the 'Reversaboard', which enables quick turns to take place in various track races. Adapted field events such as the Standing Long Jump, Vertical Jump, Speed Bounce and Soft Javelin complete the programme, thus enabling large numbers of children to experience an exciting team format whilst also learning basic skills.

MANY CHILDREN CAN DO LOTS OF ACTIVITIES IN A SMALL SPACE WHEN TIME IS LIMITED.

Initially, a format and programme of competition was developed for the 11 to 15 year age groups but it was soon realised that a complementary and more appropriate format for children in the younger age group was required. Following considerable research, consultation and early pioneering events involving touring around the United Kingdom, the concept of 'Fun In Athletics' was born which enabled athletics to be introduced to children aged 8–11 years as an exciting team game.

When applying the rules for competition in Sportshall Athletics disqualification is seen as a last resort, particularly with regard to the younger age groups. It is preferred that officials follow a policy of correction and penalties whenever possible to avoid neutralising a result.

Sportshall Athletic competitions are presented in three stages to meet the requirements of the developing child.

9.1.1 Stage One - Children Aged 8–11 years
For this age group indoor athletics is presented as a team game and referred to as 'Fun In Athletics'. All track races take on the form of relays and the field event scoring is based on Group Aggregate performances. Team sizes should be large with programmes that include lots of 'event stations' so as to provide an opportunity for the less talented. It is important for all children to fell part of the team and contribute to the overall team performance.

9.1.2 Stage Two - Children Aged 11–13 years
For this age group indoor athletics is referred to as Sportshall Athletics. This is an age when children are starting to get a little more independent and may wish to take part in their 'own' events. To meet this desire, individual events can be introduced as part of a team competition complementing the criteria given at Stage One, which still applies.

A proviso stressing that team membership is important emphasizing that if a team is to succeed its members must contribute by taking part in events other than their favourite. This proviso helps to combat event specialisation at an early age.

8.2.3 Stage Three - Children Aged 13–15 years

Competition for this age group is normally presented as a multi-event team competition and once again referred to as Sportshall Athletics. The 'All-Rounder' incorporates individual athletic ability in a multi-event environment, which is combined with practical skills and good team management. The 'All-Rounder' format helps to develop individual qualities whilst maintaining a team perspective and prepares athletes for the dual demands implicit in membership of an athletic club or other peer group.

Each team to consist of six girls and six boys with an additional one girl and one boy nominated as reserves. The six girls and six boys will compete in three events (and one relay) of which one must be from each of the following sections:

	Girls	**Boys**
Section A	2 Lap or 4 Lap	2 Lap or 4 Lap
Section B	Standing Long Jump or Vertical Jump	Standing Long Jump or Vertical Jump
Section C	Speed Bounce or Shot	Speed Bounce or Shot

- Teams are limited to three competitors in any one event.
- A girls team manager and a boys team manager must be nominated to be responsible for the teams.
- Teams must also field a 4 x 2 Lap Relay and an 8 Lap Paarlauf team (two members).
  The nominated reserve may be substituted into one of these events.
- Whenever possible the nominated reserves should be allowed to compete as a non-scoring member in the individual events.

9.2 Hall Layouts (FIA & SHA)

Example of Track Layout

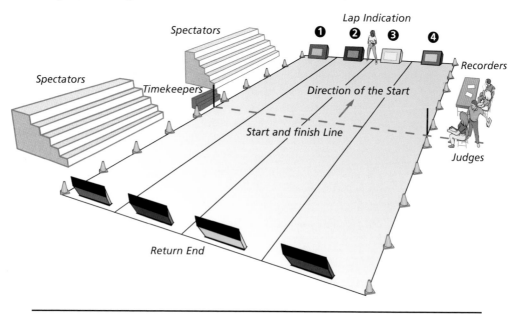

Example of Field Events Layout

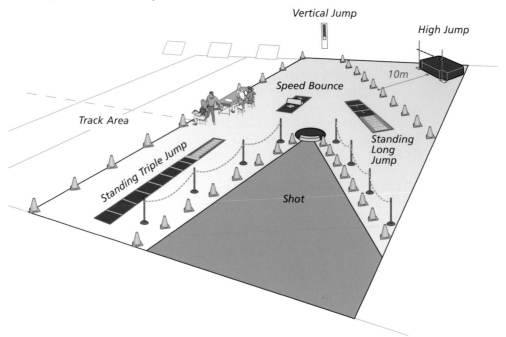

9.3 Recommended Track Events (FIA & SHA)

Events	8–11 years	11–13 years	13–15 years
Individual Races	✔	✔	✘
1 Lap Race	✔	✔	✘
2 Lap Race	✔	✔	✔
4 Lap Race	✔	✔	✔
6 Lap Race	✘	✔	✔
8 Lap Race	✘	✘	✔
Pairs and Paarlauf Races			
1 lap + 1 lap	✔	✔	✘
1 lap + 2 lap	✔	✔	✘
3 lap + 3 lap (run as time-trials)	✔	✔	✔
6 lap Paarlauf (run as time-trials)	✔	✔	✔
8 lap Paarlauf (run as time-trials)	✘	✔	✔
10 lap Paarlauf (run as time-trials)	✘	✘	✔

Children in the 8–11 years age group
should not run heats and finals for races above two laps.

For the two older age groups races above four laps
and all paarlaufs should be run as time-trials.

Relays	8–11 years	11–13 years	13–15 years
4 x 1 Lap Obstacle	✔	✔	✘
4 x 1 Lap Over / Under	✔	✔	✘
4 x 1 Lap Sprint	✔	✔	✘
4 x 1 Hurdle	✔	✔	✔
4 x 2 Lap Sprint	✔	✔	✔
4 x 2 Lap Hurdle	✘	✔	✔
Medley Relay			
4 lap / 2 lap / 2 lap / 4 lap	✘	✘	✔
Grand Prix	✔	✔	✘

Relays may be run as time-trials or heats and finals depending upon the time permitting within the programme.

Assuming the length of the gymnasium does not exceed 40 metres.

Minimum Rest Periods
Races or Relay legs having 1 or 2 Laps = 20 minutes
Races or Relay legs having 3 or 4 Laps = 30 minutes

9.3.1 Track Events for Individuals

These events always use a common start and finishing line. The races always start and finish with competitors facing the first turn board and this is the end of the gymnasium where the lap indicator cards are located so that the number of laps to be run can be clearly seen.

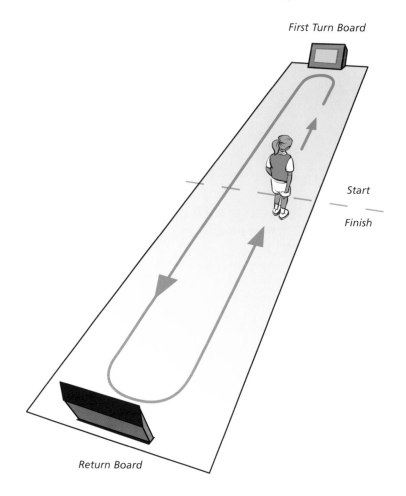

First Turn Board

Start

Finish

Return Board

Activity: The competitor turns on the first turn reversaboard and then runs the length of the gymnasium where another turn is made on the return board. The lap finishes at the starting line with the competitor facing in the same direction as he or she started. The competitor has then completed one lap, which is equivalent of running two lengths of the gymnasium. The recommended minimum lane width is 2.2 metres.

It is important to note that the length run on a sportshall track does not equate to the same distance run on an outdoor 400 metre track. This is due to the fact that the competitior will slow slightly as he or she approaches the turn and there is a short pause when turning followed by re-acceleration.

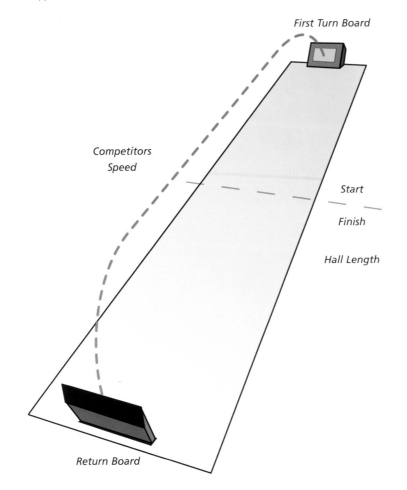

First Turn Board

Competitors Speed

Start

Finish

Hall Length

Return Board

9.3.2 Relays
9.3.2.1 Sprint Relay

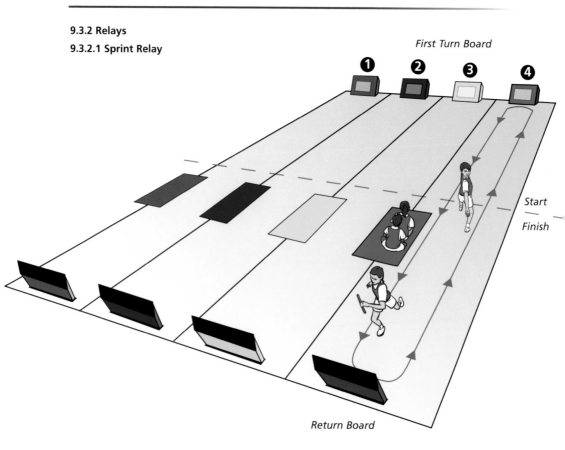

First Turn Board

Start

Finish

Return Board

Activity: A sprint relay is where team members carry a baton over a specified number of laps. The start and finish is the halfway point between the two 'reversaboards'. Waiting team members sit on their team mat to the side of their lane. A complete lap is the distance from the start / finish line to the first turn board followed by the full length of the hall to the return board and back to the start / finish line. The first runner stands behind the start line facing the first turn board. On the whistle, the first runner completes the required number of laps and passes the baton to the next team member. After exchanging the baton the runner returns to sit on the team mat and the last runner finishes the relay by crossing the start / finish line at the end of his or her final lap.

9.3.2.2 Hurdle Relay

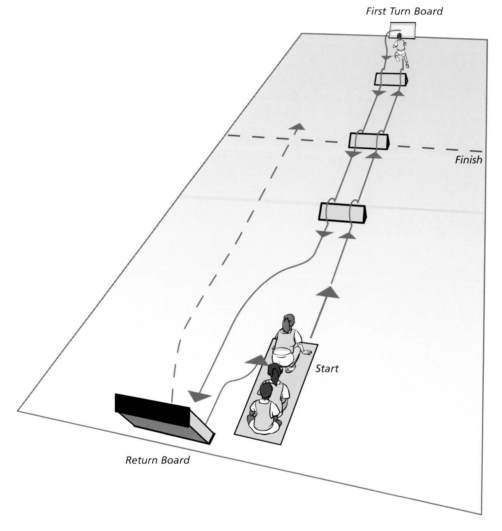

First Turn Board

Finish

Start

Return Board

Activity: Each young athlete completes one lap of the course, attempting the hurdles both on the way out and on the return. The first team member starts on the whistle and then continues over the three hurdles and turns on the first turn board. On the return run he or she repeats the course in the opposite direction and turns on the return board before touching the shoulder of the next athlete who is crouched in front of the team mat for takeover. All team members complete this sequence but the last runner must sprint to the finish line after turning on the return board.

9.3.2.3 Obstacle Relay

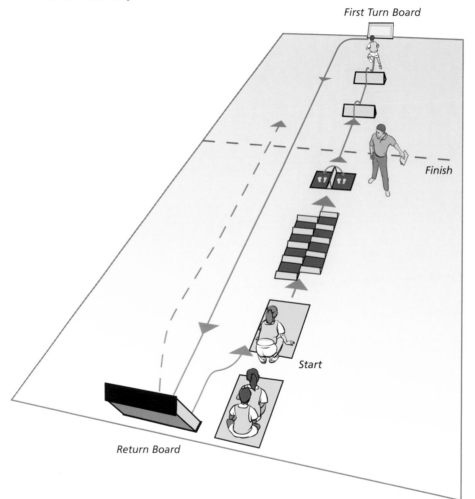

Activity: Each young athlete completes one lap of the course, attempting the obstacles on the way out and sprinting on the return. The first team member starts on the whistle with a forward roll, which should be performed from a kneeling position with both hands on the mat. He or she then completes the Hi-Stepper by placing one foot in every space, performs ten Speed Bounces with feet together over a 200mm wedge and runs over the two hurdles. After he or she turns on the first turn board. On the return run no obstacles are attempted and the young athlete must sprint back and turn on the return board before touching the shoulder of the next athlete who is crouched in front of the team mat for takeover. All team members complete this sequence but the last runner must sprint to the finish line after turning on the return board.

9.3.2.4 Over Under Relay

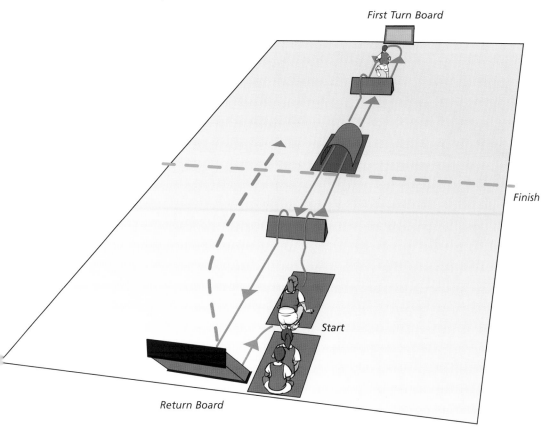

First Turn Board

Finish

Start

Return Board

Activity: Each young athlete completes one lap of the course, attempting the obstacles both on the way out and on the return. The first team member starts on the whistle with a forward roll, which should be performed from a kneeling position with both hands on the mat. He or she then continues over the hurdle, under the tunnel, over the hurdle and turns on the first turn board. On the return run the course is repeated in the opposite direction with a turn on the return board before the shoulder is touched of the next athlete who is crouched in front of the team mat for takeover. All team members complete this sequence but the last runner must sprint to the finish line after turning on the return board. This relay should only be used with young athletes aged 12 years and under.

9.3.2.5 Grand Prix Relay

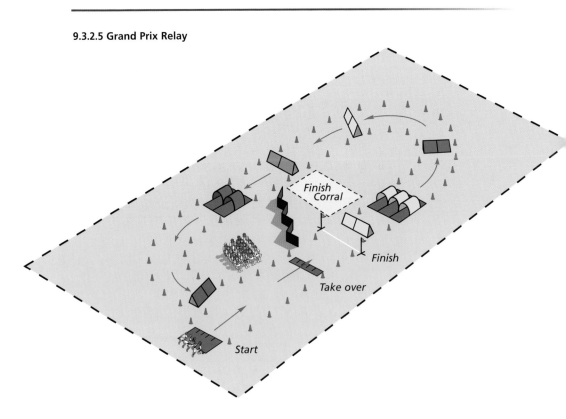

Activity: This is an exciting relay where each team member completes one lap of the grand prix circuit. The first runner starts on the whistle with a forward roll, which should be performed from a kneeling position with both hands on the mat. He or she then continues to run round the circuit over hurdles and through tunnels. The second team members are handed their team's beanbag at the takeover point and proceed round the circuit. The activity continues with all team members completing a circuit before the last runner crosses the finish line. Please note that the overall course length should not exceed 200 metres.

9.4 Recommended Field Events

The field events that are detailed in the table below have been detailed throughout other sections of the book.

Events	8–11 years	11–13 years	13–15 years
Standing Long Jump	✔	✔	✔
Standing Triple Jump	✔	✔	✔
Vertical Jump	✔	✔	✔
High Jump (10m restricted take-off)	✘	✘	✔
5 Strides	✔	✔	✔
Putting the Shot – Girls	✔ (600 g)	✔ (2.72 kg)	✔ (3.25 kg)
Putting the Shot – Boys	✔ (600 g)	✔ (3.25 kg)	✔ (4 kg)
Soft Javelin	✔	✔	✘
Speed Bounce	✔ (maximum 20 secs.)	✔ (maximum 20 secs.)	✔ (maximum 30 secs.)
Sitting Throw	✔ (size 4 soccer ball)	✔ (size 4 soccer ball)	✔ (size 4 soccer ball)
Soccer Throw – Girls	✔ (size 4 soccer ball)	✔ (1kg medicine ball)	✔ (1kg medicine ball)
Soccer Throw – Boys	✔ (size 4 soccer ball)	✔ (1kg medicine ball)	✔ (2kg medicine ball)
Chest Push – Girls	✔ (1kg medicine ball)	✔ (2kg medicine ball)	✔ (2kg medicine ball)
Chest Push – Boys	✔ (1kg medicine ball)	✔ (2kg medicine ball)	✔ (3kg medicine ball)
Overhead Heave – Girls	✘ (2kg medicine ball)	✔ (2kg medicine ball)	✔
Overhead Heave - Boys	✘ (2kg medicine ball)	✔ (3kg medicine ball)	✔
Caber	✔	✘	✘
Target Throw	✔	✘	✘

Full details of sportshall athletic events and the rules for competition are available and are published by International Fun and Team Athletics.

10.1 Introduction to Officiating - Assisting

When officiating for young athletes aged 8–13 years, the main emphasis should be placed upon fair play. The young athletes should attempt to compete by the rules but if mistakes are made it is better for the official to give penalties rather than disqualification. Officials for this age group must therefore know the rules to the event and be able to interpret the rules to fit the situation. It is a good idea to provide encouragement for the young athletes whilst they are competing, as long as this is given consistently to all. It must be made quite clear at this point that officiating for this age group and officiating for older athletes will require the application of different skills and qualities.

What you will need as an official:
- Ability to ensure safety at all times
- Ability to assess and eliminate risk
- Enthusiasm
- Knowledge of rules of the event
- Ability to work as part of a team
- Personal Equipment
    Pen, Clipboard, Stopwatch (if timekeeping), Appropriate Clothing, Flat Shoes, Fingerless Gloves and Waterproofs (for outdoor use), Rule Book and plenty of liquid refreshment.
- Awareness of emergency protocol in the event of an accident or injury.

Officiating can be a very enjoyable experience and many people start as a result of their child's involvement in athletics. It can prove to be very rewarding and a life-long hobby but it is very important to gain the appropriate qualifications.

10.2 Duties of Officials

The following sub-sections will provide useful tips to allow inexperienced helpers to assist qualified officials but it should be emphasised that any questions that arise should be addressed to qualified officials at the competition.

10.2.1 Track Judge

Track judges should be positioned on the extension of the finishing line set slightly back from the inside lane of the track. Finishing order should be recorded in a vertical column to avoid confusion between the numbers worn by the young athletes. Finishing position is based upon when the torso crosses the vertical plane of the finishing line. If different results are produced by an equal number of judges, then the decision will go to the Chief Track Judge.

200m Heat 1	200m Heat 2	200m Heat 3
16	31	12
4	22	13
19	7	2
27	11	1
3	5	25
33	6	26

A good tip when judging is to write down the anticipated finishing order before the athletes reach the finishing line. The judge can then concentrate his or her attention on the actual finish and make adjustments to the order as necessary. In the example shown above, in Heat two athlete number 11 was judged to reach the finish line before athlete number 7. In Heat three athlete number 26 was judged to have overtaken both athletes number 25 and number 1, who have also reversed in finishing order and therefore the corrected results would be:

200m Heat 1	200m Heat 2	200m Heat 3
16	31	12
4	22	13
19	11	2
27	7	26
3	5	25
33	6	1

10.2.2 Timekeeper

Timekeepers should be positioned on the extension of the finishing line set slightly back from the outside lane of the track.

a) When timekeeping it is important to have a clear vision of the starting area and be able to observe the competitors from the moment they are called to their marks.
b) Avoid distractions by field events, conversation or wandering bodies.
c) Start the watch when a flash or smoke is seen from the gun.
d) As the young athletes approach the **finish**, concentration should be fixed on the line, keeping the runners out of focus.
e) The torso of the young athlete must cut the vertical plane of the finishing line before the watch of the position being timed is stopped.
f) The watch is set back to zero only after the time has been recorded by the Chief Timekeeper.

10.2.3 Starter's Assistant

The obvious duty of the Starter's Assistant is to help the starter who is completely in charge of the start of each race and the assistant's responsibilities include the following:

1) Marshalling the young athletes.
2) Grouping the young athletes into heats if they have not been decided beforehand.
3) Ensuring young athletes are correctly attired.
4) Ensuring young athletes have their numbers pinned correctly to their running vests.
5) Ensuring young athletes are in the correct lanes for the start of the race.
6) Ensuring young athletes keep their fingers (crouch start) or toes (standing start) behind the start line.
7) Assisting the starter to observe any infringements or false starts.

10.2.4 Field Judge

There are many different roles within field judging because of the number of different field events and because each event has its own individual set of rules. Knowledge and understanding of these rules is a very important part of field judging. Therefore it is highly probable that an inexperienced field judge will not carry out decision making tasks and is more likely to be covering such duties as raking sandpits, replacing the high jump bar or collecting throwing implements. The safety of the athletes and judges is of paramount importance in field events, especially throwing, and therefore the judge should remain vigilant at all times.

11.1 Events

The 'Agility Challenge' is an Athletics Award Scheme that is based around the fundamental core motor skills and was devised by IFTA for international purposes. There are three standard 'Challenges' with the option to run individual event scores.

The standard 'Challenges' are the triathlon, pentathlon and decathlon.

11.1.1 Triathlon
The Triathlon includes the following events:
• Balance Test • Standing Long Jump • Speed Bounce

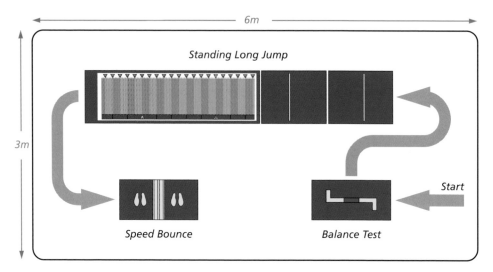

The IFTA Triathlon is the first of the 'Agility Challenges'. This simple set of three events test athletic ability over a wide skills range including coordination, balance, speed, rhythm and leg strength.

The 'Challenge' can be set up where space is limited and is designed to provide opportunities for large numbers of participants. Each young athlete should be given a personal scorecard on which his or her performances and scores are recorded. Emphasis should be on participation and self-improvement.

AGILITY CHALLENGE - TRIATHLON SCORECARD

NAME		AGE		GIRL	
				BOY	

CLASS / GROUP

EVENTS	TRIALS						PERFORMANCE	POINTS
BALANCE TEST (4x15 seconds)	LEFT LEG	RIGHT LEG		LEFT LEG	RIGHT LEG		TOTAL	
STANDING LONG JUMP	1		2		3		BEST	
SPEED BOUNCE (20 seconds)	10	20	30	40	50	60	TOTAL	
SIGNED							TOTAL POINTS	

11.1.2 Pentathlon

The Pentathlon includes the following events:

• Balance Test • Standing Long Jump • Speed Bounce • Target Throw • Hi-Stepper

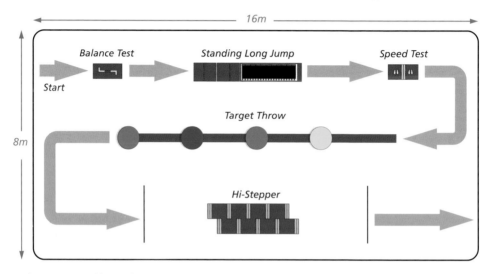

The IFTA Pentathlon is the second stage of the 'Agility Challenges' and adds two more events to the IFTA Triathlon, extending the range of skills involved to include eye to hand co-ordination, agility and throwing accuracy in addition to the existing skills of co-ordination, balance, speed, rhythm and leg strength.

The 'Challenge' can be set up where space is limited and is designed to provide opportunities for large numbers of participants. Each young athlete should once again be given a personal scorecard on which his or her performances and scores are recorded.

AGILITY CHALLENGE - PENTATHLON SCORECARD

NAME		AGE	GIRL	
			BOY	

CLASS / GROUP

EVENTS	TRIALS						PERFORMANCE	POINTS
BALANCE TEST (4x15 seconds)	LEFT LEG	RIGHT LEG	LEFT LEG	RIGHT LEG			TOTAL	
STANDING LONG JUMP	1		2		3		BEST	
SPEED BOUNCE (20 seconds)	10	20	30	40	50	60	TOTAL	
TARGET THROW	YELLOW - 3m	GREEN - 5m	BLUE - 7m	RED - 9m			TOTAL	
HI-STEPPER (4 x 8m shuttle run)	TIME TAKEN (secs)		FAULTS				ADJUSTED TIME	
SIGNED							TOTAL POINTS	

11.1.3 Decathlon

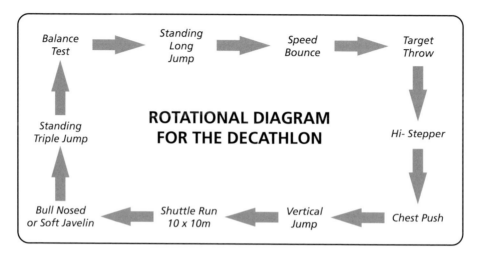

The IFTA Decathlon is suitable for larger groups of children allowing participation in a wide variety of events and skills. Where space and time are limited, individuals or teams can be organised so that they 'flow' from station-to-station as timed intervals. Young athletes may carry personal scorecards or for team competition standard event scorecards can be used. The format uses the IFTA point tables (shown in section 11.2) to calculate both individual and team scores.

The IFTA Decathlon is suitable for school sports days, club sessions and team competitions.

The Decathlon includes the following events:
• Balance Test • Standing Long Jump • Speed Bounce • Target Throw • Hi-Stepper • Chest Push
• Vertical Jump • 10 x 10 Shuttle Run • Soft Javelin • Standing Triple Jump

11.1.4 Allocating Points
Points are allocated to the young athletes depending upon the performance they achieve. Points tables have been produced for both girls and boys and can be seen in section 11.2. For example, if a girl achieves 1.66m in the Standing Long Jump she will be awarded 43 points for that performance.

11.1.5 Calculating an Award
When a young athlete has completed all the events in either the triathlon, pentathlon or decathlon and the appropriate points allocated for his or her performances, an award level can then be calculated. The Awards Tables can be seen in section 11.3 and the levels achievable range from one to seven in individual years for young athletes aged 7–15 years. For example, a young athlete aged 9 scoring 98 points in the triathlon would achieve level four or the blue level.

AGILITY CHALLENGE - DECATHLON SCORECARD

NAME					AGE		GIRL	
							BOY	

CLASS / GROUP

EVENTS	TRIALS						PERFORMANCE	POINTS
BALANCE TEST	LEFT LEG	RIGHT LEG	LEFT LEG	RIGHT LEG			TOTAL	
(4x15 seconds)								
STANDING LONG JUMP	1		2		3		BEST	
SPEED BOUNCE	10	20	30	40	50	60	TOTAL	
(20 seconds)								
TARGET THROW	YELLOW - 3m	GREEN - 5m	BLUE - 7m	RED - 9m			TOTAL	
HI-STEPPER	TIME TAKEN (secs)		FAULTS				ADJUSTED TIME	
(4 x 8m shuttle run)								
1Kg CHEST PUSH	1		2		3		BEST	
VERTICAL JUMP	1		2		3		BEST	
SHUTTLE RUN 10 x 10m	**TIME TRIAL**						SECONDS	
SOFT JAVELIN	1		2		3		BEST	
STANDING TRIPLE JUMP	1		2		3		BEST	
SIGNED							TOTAL POINTS	

11.1.6 Event Rules
Balance Test
Description

The ability to **balance** is a fundamental element of all sporting activity. IFTA has adapted the standard 'Euro-fit test' into a competition for the Agility Challenge.

The Test

Left foot	15 seconds
Right foot	15 seconds
Left foot	15 seconds
Right foot	15 seconds
Total	**60 seconds**

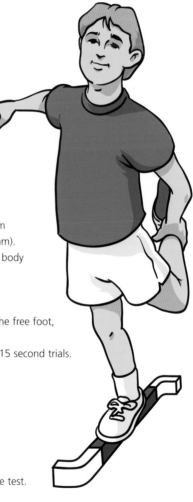

Equipment
- An IFTA approved Balance Beam
- Stopwatch
- Balance Beam Mat (optional)

Rules
- The young athlete should place one foot on the beam (this foot must be in line with and not across the beam).
- Thee free leg should be held at the ankle behind the body and balance gained by holding the judge's arm.
- The watch starts when the judge's supporting arm is released.
- The watch stops when the young athlete lets go of the free foot, touches the floor or completes 15 seconds.
- The young athlete changes legs for each of the four 15 second trials.
- The maximum time possible is 60 seconds.
- Time is recorded down to the nearest whole second.

Tips

For young athletes:
- Use free arm to aid balance.

For judges:
- Allow each young athlete to become familiar with the test.
- Allow the young athlete to gain balance by holding the judges arm prior to the start of the test.

Safety
- Ensure that the balance beam is not able to slide on the floor.
- The use of a balance beam mat is recommended.

Standing Long Jump
Description
This two footed jump from a standing position is a test of **co-ordination** and **leg strength**. In 1904 an Olympic record of 3.47m was recorded into a sand pit and it stood for over 80 years! The new world record is now over 3.60m. In IFTA events a special graduated landing mat is used which enables jumps to be recorded more easily.

Equipment
- A Standing Long Jump Mat

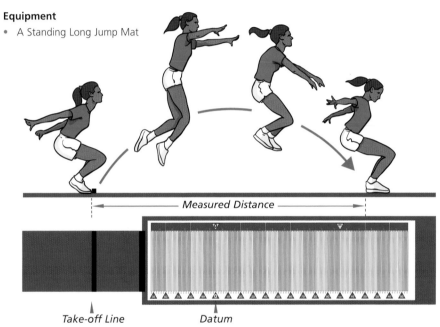

Rules
- A two footed take off from a standing position with both feet behind the take-off line.
- Measurement is taken from the take off line to the back of the closest heel on landing.
- The young athlete may step forward after the jump however **any step back or touching of the mat behind the feet is a no jump.**

Tips
For young athletes:
- Bend at the knees and swing arms for lift.

For judges:
- Place a finger on the scale where the young athlete lands then read the result.

Safety
- Keep landing area away from obstructions such as walls.
- Avoid water or dirt on surfaces.

Speed Bounce

Description

A test of **speed, rhythm and co-ordination** the athlete crosses the foam wedge with both feet as many times as possible in the allocated time limit.

IFTA Agility Challenge test period

All ages – 20 seconds

Equipment

- An IFTA approved Speed Bounce Mat
- Stopwatch
- Whistle

Rules

- The young athlete is allowed one trial over the allocated test period.
- The young athlete starts on the mat with both feet together to one side of the wedge.
- Starting on the whistle the young athlete must complete as many bounces as possible within the time limit.
- Both feet must touch each side of the mat for each bounce to count.
- A bounce is considered void if the wedge is jumped on.
- If the wedge is touched but both the young athletes feet still cross to the other side then the bounce is counted.
- The test finishes on the whistle.

Tips

For judges:

- Two judges are recommended, one for the timing and one to count the correct bounces.
- Allow a practise period for the participants to become familiar with the test.
- From experience it has been observed that counting in increments of two i.e. 2,4,6,8,10 ensures greater accuracy because the young athletes feet must always be on the same side of the wedge in sequence with the even count. Counting in single figures often gets out of sequence.

Safety

- Young athletes should wear suitable shoes that are fastened securely.
- The mat can be prevented from slipping by the judge placing a foot on its corner.

Target Throw

Description

The **target throw** is a test of **hand to eye co-ordination** and **throwing accuracy**. The young athlete throws coloured bean bags into the same coloured targets at distances of 3, 5, 7 and 9 metres.

Equipment
- Twenty Bean Bags (5 x yellow, green, blue and red)
- Four Target Hoops (80cm diameter with backboards 12.5cm high)
- Graduated Measuring Mat (with velcro).

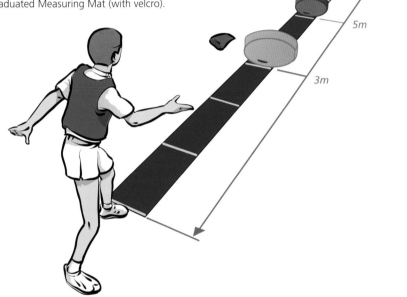

Rules
- Standing behind the throwing line the young athlete throws five matching coloured bean bags into the nearest target and continues for each different coloured target.
- Two points are scored if the bean bag lands **directly** in the same coloured target.
- One point is scored if the bean bag touches the floor before ending up in the target or if the bean bag lands only partly in the target.
- No points are scored if the bean bags land in a different coloured target, or bounces out of the target. (maximum score is 40).

Tips

For young athletes:
- Place the opposite leg to the throwing arm forward to assist balance.

For judges:
- A stopper board or gym bench can be used to prevent young athletes from stepping over the throwing line.

I·F·T·A

Hi-Stepper
Description
Inspired by the tyres American footballer's use for training, the IFTA **Hi-Stepper test** is an explosive event that develops **agility, co-ordination, speed** and **acceleration**. During a timed 8 metre shuttle run the young athlete must pass through the Hi-Stepper four times.

Equipment
- An IFTA approved Hi-Stepper
- Four Cones
- Marker Tape
- Stopwatch

Start/Finish

8m

Return Line

Rules
- The young athlete starts from behind the start line and sprints over the Hi-Stepper placing one foot in each of the spaces.
- The young athlete then places one foot **over** the return line before turning and repeating the Hi-Stepper in the other direction.
- After completing the Hi-Stepper four times the clock is stopped when the start line is re-crossed.
- Time is taken to the nearest tenth of a second.
- Time penalties of 0.2 seconds are added for missing spaces or stepping onto wedges.
- For turning short of the line a penalty of 0.2 seconds per turn is added, providing the short fall is not excessive.

Tips
For young athletes:
- Make sure that you do the Hi-Stepper correctly to avoid time penalties.
For judges:
- Two cones on the start and return lines provide a focus for young athletes and judges.

Safety
- Ensure adequate run off at each ends of the Hi-Stepper.

Chest Push

Description

In this standing throw the young athlete pushes a 1kg ball with both hands from the chest into a pre-measured throwing area. This is a good introduction the push technique used in the shot putt event. This technique is also used in Basketball and Net Ball where it is known as the chest pass.

Equipment

- 1kg Medicine Ball
- 10m Graduated Measuring Mat

Rules

- The ball is held against the chest and must be pushed with both hands.
- Both feet must remain on the floor at all times.
- One foot may be in front of the other however no run up or steps are permitted.
- The young athlete must not pass the throw line.
- Measurement is to the point the ball first touches the floor reading down to the nearest 25cm band.
- The young athletes chest must face forward at all times during the throw, trunk rotation techniques are not allowed.

Tips

For young athletes:

- Bend knees and straighten in time with throwing the ball to aid with power. For optimum performance release the ball at 45 degrees.

For judges:

- Stand to the side of the throwing area and read distance from the graduated measuring mat.

Safety

- Wherever possible throw towards a wall.

I·F·T·A

Vertical Jump
Description

A jump from a standing position in which the young athlete competes against their own height and weight. The vertical jump is an internationally recognised measurement of fitness testing leg strength to body weight ratio. The IFTA event uses a magnetically held sliding scale, which is adjusted to the young athlete's height before each jump.

Equipment
- A Vertical Jump Scale
- Chalk Bag
- Cleaning Cloth

Rules
- The young athlete stands with their back, head   and heels touching the wall.
- Both arms are stretched upwards to push the slider up with the fingertips.
- Elbows and fingers must be straight, arms must touch the side of the head and both feet must be flat on the floor.
- The young athlete dips their finger tips in chalk and jumps from a standing position.
- The young athlete touches the scale at the highest point they can.
- Measurement should be taken to the nearest centimetre below the top of the chalk mark on the scale.

Tips

For young athletes:
- Stand side on to the jump scale bend both knees and swing arms for lift to take off.

For judges:
- Use a cloth to clean chalk from the sliding scale. Talc is a good substitute for chalk. Pull the sliding scale down to record the exact height of the jump.

Safety
- Chalk on floors can cause slips ensure excess chalk is cleaned up.

Shuttle Run
Description
A timed sprint over a 10m course, the young athlete is tested on their ability to **accelerate**, **decelerate** and change direction by running up and down the course to complete ten lengths.

Equipment
- Four Cones
- Stopwatch
- Whistle
- Tape

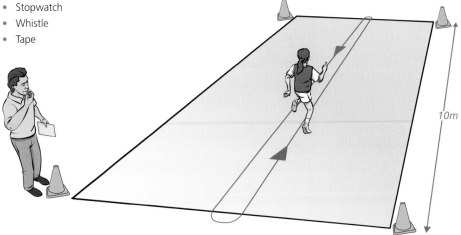

Rules
- The 10m course is laid out as shown in the diagram.
- The young athlete is started from a standing position with the blowing of a whistle and must complete the 10m distance ten times before crossing the finish line.
- The young athlete must place one foot over the end of each 10m run line before turning to run in the opposite direction.

Safety
- Ensure that running surface is suitable, free from debris and there is an adequate run off area at each end of the course.

Soft Javelin

Description

A standing throw using a foam or bull nosed javelin the event takes place on a pre-marked throwing area. This is a linear throw where distance is recorded in metres by reading across to the scale.

Equipment

- IFTA approved Foam Javelins (indoor)
- IFTA approved Bull Nosed Javelins (outdoor)
- 10m Graduated Measuring Mats
- Cones

Rules

- The javelin is thrown from a standing position with both feet being behind the throwing line and in contact with the floor.
- The throw is measured from the front of the throwing line to where the tip of the javelin first hits the ground by reading at right angles to the graduated measuring mats.
- The distance is measured in complete metres cleared by the throw. The measurement is always rounded down to the metre below where the tip contact is made.

Tips

For young athletes:

- The correct place to hold the javelin is the point where it balances when laid across the open palm of the hand.
- Place the opposite leg to the throwing arm forward for the correct stance.

For judges:

- Three judges are recommended.
- Judge one observes the young athlete at the throwing line and records the distance.
- Judges two and three make a decision on the landing position of the javelin tip to the nearest complete metre below the distance thrown.

Safety

- All throwing activity must be properly supervised.
- The throwing area should be clearly isolated using barriers or cones to prevent non-competitors or spectators walking into it.
- Never allow the javelin to be thrown back to waiting young athletes. IFTA javelins are designed to be safe, but it is important to teach good practice at an early age.

Standing Triple Jump
Description
A hop, step and jump from a standing position. The triple jump mat has take off lines at metre intervals. The athlete starts their jump from the line that enables them to land on the Graduated landing scale.

Equipment
• An IFTA approved Standing Triple Jump Mat

Rules
• A one footed take off starts a hop, step and jump sequence that must be correctly performed.
• The young athlete may crouch or rock before the jump but the leading front foot must not break contact with the ground before the start of the jump (this does not apply to the back foot).
• Measurement is from the take off line to the back of the closest heel on landing of the jump.
• The young athlete may step forward after the jump, however **any step back or touching of the mat behind the feet is a no jump**.
• Each young athlete is allowed one trial jump to enable him or her to nominate a starting point in agreement with the Judge.

Tips
For young athletes:
Those who find the sequence difficult to learn the following technique is useful:
• Hold the free leg to make the hop then let go of this leg and step on the opposite foot, then jump to land on both feet.
For judges:
• Place a finger on the scale where the young athlete lands then read the result.

Safety
• Keep landing area away from obstructions such as walls.
• Avoid water or dirt on surfaces.

I·F·T·A

11.2 Points Tables

Girls 1A

If your score goes off the table points are awarded as follows:

Points	Balance Test 4 x 15 secs	Standing Long Jump	Speed Bounce 20 secs	Target Throw	Hi-Stepper 4 x 8m	Chest Push 1kg	Vertical Jump	Shuttle Run 10 x 10m	Soft or Bull Nosed Javelin	Standing Triple Jump	Points
increments	n/a	2cm	1 no.	n/a	0.1 Sec	25cms	1cm	0.1 Sec	1 mtrs	6cm	increments
Points	n/a	1	1	n/a	2	2	1	1	2	1	Points
	secs	mtrs	no.	no.	secs	mtrs	cms	secs	mtrs	mtrs	
80	-	2.52	73	-	11.5	11.75	68	23.4	-	7.60	80
79	-	2.50	72	-	11.6	-	67	23.6	30	7.53	79
78	-	2.48	71	-	11.7	11.50	66	23.8	-	7.46	78
77	-	2.46	70	-	11.8	-	65	23.9	29	7.39	77
76	-	2.44	69	-	11.9	11.25	64	24.0	-	7.32	76
75	-	2.42	68	40	12.0	-	63	24.1	28	7.25	75
74	-	2.40	67	39	12.2	11.00	62	24.2	-	7.18	74
73	-	2.37	66	-	12.4	-	61	24.3	27	7.11	73
72	-	2.34	65	38	12.5	10.75	-	24.4	-	7.04	72
71	60	2.32	64	37	12.6	-	60	24.5	26	6.97	71
70	-	2.30	63	-	12.7	10.50	59	24.6	-	6.90	70
69	59	2.28	62	36	12.8	-	-	24.7	25	6.83	69
68	-	2.26	61	35	12.9	10.25	58	24.8	-	6.76	68
67	58	2.24	60	-	13.0	-	57	24.9	24	6.69	67
66	57	2.22	59	34	13.1	10.00	-	25.0	-	6.62	66
65	56	2.20	58	33	13.2	9.75	56	25.1	23	6.55	65
64	55	2.18	57	-	13.3	9.50	55	25.2	-	6.48	64
63	54	2.16	-	32	13.4	-	-	25.3	-	6.42	63
62	53	2.14	56	31	13.5	9.25	54	25.4	22	6.36	62
61	52	2.12	55	-	13.6	-	53	25.5	-	6.30	61
60	51	2.10	-	30	13.7	9.00	-	25.6	-	6.24	60
59	50	2.08	54	-	13.8	-	52	25.7	21	6.18	59
58	49	2.06	53	29	13.9	8.75	51	25.8	-	6.12	58
57	48	2.03	-	-	14.0	8.50	-	25.9	-	6.06	57
56	47	2.00	52	28	14.1	8.25	50	26.0	20	6.00	56
55	46	1.97	51	-	14.2	8.00	49	26.3	-	5.93	55
54	45	1.94	-	27	14.3	-	48	26.6	-	5.86	54
53	44	1.91	50	-	14.4	7.75	47	26.9	19	5.79	53
52	43	1.88	-	26	14.5	7.50	46	27.2	-	5.72	52
51	42	1.85	49	25	14.6	-	45	27.5	-	5.64	51
50	41	1.82	-	24	14.7	7.25	44	27.8	18	5.56	50
49	40	1.79	48	23	14.8	7.00	43	28.1	-	5.48	49
48	39	1.76	-	22	14.9	-	42	28.4	17	5.40	48
47	38	1.74	47	21	15.0	6.75	41	28.7	-	5.32	47
46	37	1.72	-	20	15.1	6.50	40	29.0	16	5.24	46
45	36	1.70	46	19	15.2	-	-	29.3	-	5.18	45
44	35	1.68	-	18	15.3	6.25	39	29.6	15	5.14	44
43	34	1.66	45	17	15.4	-	38	29.9	-	5.10	43
42	33	1.64	44	16	15.5	6.00	-	30.1	14	5.05	42
41	32	1.62	43	15	15.6	-	37	30.3	-	5.00	41

Girls 1B

Points	Balance Test 4 x 15 secs	Standing Long Jump	Speed Bounce 20 secs	Target Throw	Hi-Stepper 4 x 8m	Chest Push 1kg	Vertical Jump	Shuttle Run 10 x 10m	Soft or Bull Nosed Javelin	Standing Triple Jump	Points
	secs	mtrs	no.	no.	secs	mtrs	cms	secs	mtrs	mtrs	
40	31	1.60	42	14	15.7	5.75	36	30.5	-	4.95	40
39	30	1.58	41	-	15.8	-	-	30.6	13	4.90	39
38	29	1.56	40	13	15.9	5.50	35	30.7	-	4.85	38
37	28	-	39	-	16.0	-	34	30.8	-	4.80	37
36	27	1.54	38	12	16.1	5.25	-	30.9	12	4.75	36
35	26	-	37	-	16.2	-	33	31.0	-	4.70	35
34	25	1.52	36	-	16.3	-	32	31.1	-	4.65	34
33	24	-	35	11	16.4	5.00	-	31.2	11	4.60	33
32	23	1.50	34	-	16.5	-	31	31.4	-	4.55	32
31	22	-	33	-	16.6	4.75	30	31.6	-	4.51	31
30	21	1.48	32	10	16.7	-	29	31.8	10	4.47	30
29	20	-	31	-	16.8	-	-	32.0	-	4.44	29
28	19	1.46	30	-	17.0	4.50	28	32.2	-	4.40	28
27	18	-	29	9	17.2	-	27	32.4	9	4.37	27
26	17	1.44	28	-	17.4	-	26	32.6	-	4.34	26
25	-	-	27	-	17.6	4.25	-	32.8	-	4.31	25
24	16	1.42	26	8	17.9	-	25	33.0	8	4.27	24
23	-	1.40	-	-	18.2	-	24	33.3	-	4.22	23
22	15	1.38	25	-	18.5	4.00	23	33.6	-	4.17	22
21	-	1.36	24	7	18.8	-	-	34.0	-	4.10	21
20	14	1.34	23	-	19.1	-	22	34.4	7	4.05	20
19	-	1.32	22	-	19.4	3.75	-	34.8	-	4.00	19
18	13	1.30	-	6	19.8	-	21	35.2	-	3.93	18
17	-	1.28	21	-	20.2	-	-	35.6	-	3.87	17
16	12	1.26	20	-	20.6	3.50	20	36.0	6	3.80	16
15	-	1.24	19	5	21.0	-	19	36.5	-	3.75	15
14	11	1.22	18	-	21.5	-	18	37.0	-	3.68	14
13	-	1.20	17	-	22.0	3.25	17	37.5	-	3.62	13
12	10	1.18	16	4	22.5	-	16	38.2	5	3.56	12
11	9	1.16	15	-	23.0	-	15	38.9	-	3.50	11
10	8	1.14	14	-	23.5	3.00	14	39.5	-	3.40	10
9	7	1.12	13	3	24.0	-	13	40.0	-	3.35	9
8	6	1.10	12	-	24.5	2.75	12	41.0	4	3.30	8
7	5	1.05	11	-	25.0	-	11	42.0	-	3.15	7
6	-	1.00	10	2	25.5	2.50	10	43.0	-	3.05	6
5	4	0.90	9	-	26.0	-	9	44.0	-	2.70	5
4	-	0.80	8	-	26.5	2.00	8	45.0	3	2.40	4
3	3	0.70	6	1	27.0	-	7	46.0	-	2.10	3
2	-	0.50	4	-	28.0	-	6	48.0	-	1.80	2
1	2	0.30	3	-	30.0	1.50	4	50.0	2	1.50	1

I·F·T·A

Boys 1A

If your score goes off the table points are awarded as follows:

Points	Balance Test 4 x 15 secs	Standing Long Jump	Speed Bounce 20 secs	Target Throw	Hi-Stepper 4 x 8m	Chest Push 1kg	Vertical Jump	Shuttle Run 10 x 10m	Soft or Bull Nosed Javelin	Standing Triple Jump	Points
increments	n/a	2cm	1 no.	n/a	0.1 Sec	25cms	1cm	0.1 Sec	1 mtrs	6cm	increments
Points	n/a	1	1	n/a	2	2	1	1	2	1	Points
	secs	mtrs	no.	no.	secs	mtrs	cms	secs	mtrs	mtrs	
80	-	2.65	73	-	11.2	12.50	70	23.0	38	8.17	80
79	-	2.62	72	-	11.3	-	69	23.1	-	8.13	79
78	-	2.59	71	-	11.4	12.25	68	23.2	37	8.08	78
77	-	2.56	70	-	11.5	-	67	23.3	36	8.03	77
76	-	2.53	69	-	11.6	12.00	66	23.4	-	7.97	76
75	-	2.50	68	40	11.7	-	65	23.5	35	7.90	75
74	-	2.48	67	39	11.8	11.75	64	23.7	34	7.82	74
73	-	2.46	66	-	12.0	-	63	23.8	-	7.74	73
72	-	2.44	65	38	12.1	11.50	62	23.9	33	7.66	72
71	60	2.42	64	37	12.2	-	61	24.0	32	7.58	71
70	-	2.40	63	-	12.3	11.25	-	24.2	-	7.50	70
69	59	2.38	62	36	12.4	-	60	24.4	31	7.42	69
68	-	2.36	61	35	12.5	11.00	59	24.5	30	7.34	68
67	58	2.34	60	-	12.6	-	58	24.6	-	7.26	67
66	57	2.32	59	34	12.7	10.75	57	24.7	29	7.18	66
65	56	2.30	58	33	12.8	-	56	24.9	-	7.10	65
64	55	2.28	57	-	13.0	10.50	55	25.0	28	7.02	64
63	54	2.26	-	32	13.1	-	-	25.1	-	6.94	63
62	53	2.24	56	31	13.2	10.25	54	25.2	27	6.86	62
61	52	2.22	55	-	13.3	10.00	53	25.3	-	6.78	61
60	51	2.20	-	30	13.4	-	-	25.4	26	6.70	60
59	50	2.17	54	-	13.5	9.75	52	25.5	-	6.62	59
58	49	2.14	53	29	13.6	9.50	51	25.6	25	6.54	58
57	48	2.11	-	-	13.7	-	-	25.7	-	6.46	57
56	47	2.08	52	28	13.8	9.25	50	25.8	24	6.38	56
55	46	2.04	51	-	14.0	9.00	49	26.0	-	6.30	55
54	45	2.01	-	27	14.1	-	48	26.3	23	6.22	54
53	44	1.99	50	-	14.2	8.75	47	26.6	-	6.14	53
52	43	1.96	-	26	14.3	8.50	46	26.8	22	6.06	52
51	42	1.93	49	25	14.4	-	45	27.0	-	6.00	51
50	41	1.90	-	24	14.5	8.25	44	27.3	21	5.94	50
49	40	1.88	48	23	14.6	8.00	43	27.6	-	5.87	49
48	39	1.85	-	22	14.7	-	42	28.0	20	5.80	48
47	38	1.82	47	21	14.8	7.75	41	28.3	-	5.74	47
46	37	1.80	-	20	15.0	7.50	40	28.6	19	5.66	46
45	36	1.77	46	19	15.1	7.25	-	29.0	-	5.60	45
44	35	1.74	-	18	15.2	7.00	39	29.3	18	5.54	44
43	34	1.70	45	17	15.3	-	38	29.6	-	5.46	43
42	33	1.68	44	16	15.4	6.75	-	29.8	17	5.38	42
41	32	1.66	43	15	15.5	6.50	37	30.0	-	5.30	41

Boys 1B

Points	Balance Test 4 x 15 secs	Standing Long Jump	Speed Bounce 20 secs	Target Throw	Hi-Stepper 4 x 8m	Chest Push 1kg	Vertical Jump	Shuttle Run 10 x 10m	Soft or Bull Nosed Javelin	Standing Triple Jump	Points
	secs	mtrs	no.	no.	secs	mtrs	cms	secs	mtrs	mtrs	
40	31	1.64	42	14	15.7	-	36	30.2	16	5.22	40
39	30	1.61	41	-	15.8	6.25	-	30.4	-	5.15	39
38	29	1.59	40	13	15.9	6.00	35	30.5	15	5.07	38
37	28	-	39	-	16.0	-	34	30.7	-	5.00	37
36	27	1.56	38	12	16.1	5.75	-	30.8	14	4.94	36
35	26	-	37	-	16.2	-	33	30.9	-	4.88	35
34	25	1.54	36	-	16.3	5.50	32	31.0	13	4.82	34
33	24	-	35	11	16.4	-	-	31.1	-	4.76	33
32	23	1.52	34	-	16.5	5.25	31	31.3	-	4.70	32
31	22	-	33	-	16.6	-	30	31.5	12	4.64	31
30	21	1.50	32	10	16.7	5.00	29	31.8	-	4.58	30
29	20	-	31	-	16.8	-	-	32.0	-	4.52	29
28	19	1.48	30	-	17.0	-	28	32.2	11	4.48	28
27	18	1.46	29	9	17.2	4.75	27	32.4	-	4.44	27
26	17	1.44	28	-	17.4	-	26	32.6	-	4.40	26
25	-	1.43	27	-	17.6	-	-	32.8	10	4.36	25
24	16	1.42	26	8	17.9	4.50	25	33.0	-	4.32	24
23	-	1.40	-	-	18.2	-	24	33.3	-	4.28	23
22	15	1.38	25	-	18.5	4.25	23	33.6	9	4.24	22
21	-	1.36	24	7	18.8	-	-	34.0	-	4.20	21
20	14	1.34	23	-	19.1	-	22	34.4	-	4.16	20
19	-	1.32	22	-	19.4	4.00	-	34.8	8	4.12	19
18	13	1.30	-	6	19.8	-	21	35.2	-	4.08	18
17	-	1.28	21	-	20.2	3.75	-	35.6	-	4.04	17
16	12	1.26	20	-	20.6	-	20	36.0	7	4.00	16
15	-	1.24	19	5	21.0	3.50	19	36.5	-	3.92	15
14	11	1.22	18	-	21.5	-	18	37.0	-	3.84	14
13	-	1.20	17	-	22.0	-	17	37.5	6	3.76	13
12	10	1.18	16	4	22.5	3.25	16	38.2	-	3.68	12
11	9	1.16	15	-	23.0	-	15	38.9	-	3.60	11
10	8	1.14	14	-	23.5	3.00	14	39.5	5	3.50	10
9	7	1.12	13	3	24.0	-	13	40.0	-	3.40	9
8	6	1.10	12	-	24.5	2.75	12	41.0	-	3.30	8
7	5	1.05	11	-	25.0	-	11	42.0	4	3.17	7
6	-	1.00	10	2	25.5	2.50	10	43.0	-	3.05	6
5	4	0.90	9	-	26.0	-	9	44.0	-	2.70	5
4	-	0.80	8	-	26.5	2.00	8	45.0	3	2.40	4
3	3	0.70	6	1	27.0	-	7	46.0	-	2.10	3
2	-	0.50	4	-	28.0	-	6	48.0	-	1.80	2
1	2	0.30	3	-	30.0	1.50	4	50.0	2	1.50	1

11.3 Awards Tables

AWARDS FOR IFTA AGILITY CHALLENGE								TRIATHLON		
AWARD COLOUR	AWARD LEVEL	AGE IN YEARS ON DAY								
		7	8	9	10	11	12	13	14	15
GOLD	7	115	126	136	145	152	158	163	168	172
SILVER	6	106	116	125	134	140	146	150	155	158
BRONZE	5	97	106	115	122	128	133	137	141	145
BLUE	4	78	86	93	99	104	108	112	115	118
GREEN	3	61	66	72	76	80	83	86	88	91
YELLOW	2	35	40	45	50	55	60	64	67	70
ORANGE	1	10	15	20	25	30	-	-	-	-

AWARDS FOR IFTA AGILITY CHALLENGE								PENTATHLON		
AWARD COLOUR	AWARD LEVEL	AGE IN YEARS ON DAY								
		7	8	9	10	11	12	13	14	15
GOLD	7	182	199	215	229	240	249	257	265	272
SILVER	6	167	183	198	211	221	229	237	244	251
BRONZE	5	153	168	181	193	202	209	216	223	229
BLUE	4	125	136	147	157	164	170	176	181	186
GREEN	3	96	105	113	121	126	131	135	139	143
YELLOW	2	66	72	78	83	87	90	93	96	99
ORANGE	1	16	25	33	40	50	-	-	-	-

AWARDS FOR IFTA AGILITY CHALLENGE								DECATHLON		
AWARD COLOUR	AWARD LEVEL	AGE IN YEARS ON DAY								
		7	8	9	10	11	12	13	14	15
GOLD	7	357	391	422	450	472	490	506	521	534
SILVER	6	329	360	389	414	435	451	466	480	492
BRONZE	5	301	329	355	379	397	413	426	439	450
BLUE	4	244	268	289	308	323	335	346	356	365
GREEN	3	188	206	222	237	248	258	266	274	281
YELLOW	2	129	141	152	163	171	177	183	189	193
ORANGE	1	30	45	60	75	90	-	-	-	-

11.4 Other Items Available

The Agility Challenge detailed within this section is aimed at the Primary Age Group (7–11 years) although can be performed by young athletes in the Secondary Age Group (12–15 years). IFTA, however has separate Triathlon, Pentathlon and Decathlon Agility Challenges for the Secondary Age Group that have adapted events to suit the needs of the older athlete.

An IFTA Agility Challenge computerised scoring package and Triathlon, Pentathlon and Decathlon certificates are available for purchase from IFTA offices. For your nearest IFTA office, please check the website which can be found at:

www.teamathletics.net

or for more information please e-mail:

awards@teamathletics.net

Other Publications available from
International Fun and Team Athletics

International Fun & Team Athletics
for the
Primary Age Group
by
George Bunner MBE

Published by International Fun and Team Athletics
Cheshire, England

ISBN 0-9542412-0-7